USTIN STREET
WARREN ST
Old Rutherford Ave
Union St
Prett St
Chelsea
Washington Street

99 / 38

Constitution
Museum

National
Historical
Park

8th Street

arbor

LEONARD P. ZAKIM BUNKER HILL MEMORIAL BRIDGE

Bunker Hill
Pavilion

HILL TO
STOWN
th Point
Park

Paul Revere
Park

New Charles
River Dam

CONSTITUTION ROAD

CHARLESTOWN BRIDGE

COMMERCIAL STREET
Copp's Hill
Burying Ground

Old North
Church

Sumner Tunnel Toll
Callahan Tunnel

NASHUA
STREET

TD Boston
Garden

BOSTON
NORTH
STATION

North Station

CAUSEWAY

Prince St

Charter St

Snow Hill St

Salem St

NORTH END

Paul Revere
Statue

Hanover Ave

ATLANTIC AVENUE

Harris St

Clark St

MARTHA ROAD

ST END

LOMASNEY WAY

Federal
Building

HAVERHILL

Portland Street

Friend Street

Lancaster Street

N WASHINGTON ST

Portal Park

Salem Street

Hull St

Fleet St

Lewis St

Eastern Ave

MERRIMAC STREET

WM Cardinal

State Service
Center

Haymarket

Paul Revere
House

Cross Street

Fulton

Commercial Street

Blossom
Court

Stanford Street

Charon Street

Government
Center

North
End
Park

North Street

P

Harrison Gray
Otis House

STREET

CAMBRIDGE

Sudbury Street

New City Hall
Government
Center

James Curley
Statues

Christopher Columbus
Waterfront Park

of African
n History
sburg
are

State
Office
Buildings

Bowdoin

Ashburton Place

New England
Holocaust
Memorial

Samuel Adams
Statue

Rose Fitzgerald Kennedy
Greenway
Wharf District

Long
Wharf

Ames
Building

Corn St

Faneuil
Marketplace

State House

Myrtle St

Derne St

King's Chapel and
Burying Ground

Faneuil
Hall

STATE STREET

Custom
House
Tower

Aquarium

Nichols
House
Museum

Boston
Athenaeum

Old State
House

P

New England
Aquarium

Robert Gould
Shaw Memorial

Granary
Burying
Ground

Old South
Meeting House

Milk St

Post Office
Square

Franklin Street

PEARL

Park Street
Church

Irish Famine
Memorial
Adams
Gallery

BOSTON COMMON
TO THE WATERFRONT

Park St

WINTER

TREE

FRANKLIN

Boston
Common

Temple Pl

FINANCIAL
DISTRICT

OTIS ST

P

Boylston

TREMONT

Downtown
Crossing

SUMMER

High

ATLANTIC

EVELYN MOAKLEY
BRIDGE

NORTHERN AVENUE

SEAPORT BOULEVARD

STREET

WASHINGTON

Avery

Bedford St

South
Station

Congress St

Boston
Children's
Museum

Colonial
Theatre

CHINATOWN

BEACH

ESSEX ST

Lincoln Street

CONGRESS STREET

Cutler Majestic
Theatre

ESSEX STREET

BOSTON
SOUTH
STATION

Boston
Tea Party
Ships and
Museum

Boston Fire
Museum

Shubert
Theatre

KNEELAND
STREET

Bus
Terminal

SUMMER ST
BRIDGE

CONGRESS STREET

SUMMER

THEATER
DISTRICT

TYLER

TREMONT

CHARLES

Wang
Center
ST

OAK

Tufts
Medical
Center

DORCHESTER AVENUE

A STREET

ROAD

HAUL

HERALD

SHAWNUT

WASHINGTON

Marginal
Road

Necco St

Sleeper St

Boston Convention and
Exhibition Center

J   K   L

BOSTON

How to Use This Book

KEY TO SYMBOLS

➕ Map reference to the accompanying fold-out map

✉ Address

☎ Telephone number

🕐 Opening/closing times

🍴 Restaurant or café

🚉 Nearest rail station

Ⓜ Nearest Metro (subway) station

🚌 Nearest bus route

🚢 Nearest riverboat or ferry stop

♿ Facilities for visitors with disabilities

❓ Other practical information

▷ Further information

ℹ Tourist information

✋ Admission charges: Expensive (over \$9), Moderate (\$4–\$9) and Inexpensive (\$3 or less)

This guide is divided into four sections

● Essential Boston: An introduction to the city and tips on making the most of your stay.
● Boston by Area: We've divided the city into five areas, and recommended the best sights, shops, entertainment venues, nightlife and restaurants in each one. Suggested walks help you to explore on foot.
● Where to Stay: The best hotels, whether you're looking for luxury, budget or something in between.
● Need to Know: The info you need to make your trip run smoothly, including getting about by public transportation, weather tips, emergency phone numbers and useful websites.

Navigation In the Boston by Area chapter, we've given each area its own color, which is also used on the locator maps throughout the book and the map on the inside front cover.

Maps The fold-out map with this book is a comprehensive street plan of Boston. The grid on this fold-out map is the same as the grid on the locator maps within the book. We've given grid references within the book for each sight and listing.

CONTENTS

Introducing Boston

While Boston's long and storied history is never forgotten—indeed, it is revered and embraced—the city always has an eye on the future, with creative innovators applying themselves to everything from cutting-edge cuisine to high tech.

Massachusetts has led many of the country's most important movements—public education, the abolition of slavery, women's equality and gay rights. Boston and Cambridge, its sister city across the Charles River (in this book, references to Boston include Cambridge), have been at the forefront of these campaigns.

The city's dedication to culture and learning is well known, and can be seen in its world-class museums, concert halls and libraries, and in the countless college campuses. Even the music venues, galleries and movie theaters have their own histories.

Meanwhile, Boston's quality of life is equally high out of doors. The string of parks and public spaces designed by Frederick Law Olmsted (collectively known as the Emerald Necklace) runs through the city, providing stunning and well-maintained green spaces in many a neighborhood. Water is almost always nearby or visible, from the Charles River Esplanade of Back Bay to the Downtown area bordering Boston Harbor. And Boston's architecture is some of the most beautiful in the country: As often as not, Victorian brownstones share blocks with art deco buildings and contemporary skyscrapers.

Of course, none of these perks comes cheap. Boston's real estate is some of the most expensive in the country, and is seemingly ever on the rise. That's largely because, unlike many American cities, Boston has made urban living desirable, so its residents are willing to spend what's necessary to live there. All in all, there are few cities in America more worth taking up residence in—or visiting.

FACTS AND FIGURES

- The "T" was the first subway system in the US. The first section opened in 1897.
- Boston Common was the first public park in America.
- Harvard University was the first college in North America.
- The nickname "Beantown" probably came from the popularity of baked beans cooked in molasses among early residents.

ODD FACTS

- Some 58 percent of Boston is built on landfill.
- Boston Light, on Little Brewster Island, was the first lighthouse in the United States (1716). It is still in operation.
- The Boston University Bridge is the only place in the world where a boat can sail under a train driving under a car driving under a plane.

LOCAL PASSIONS

● Don't be surprised if locals give directions using ubiquitous Dunkin' Donuts as landmarks; it seems like there's one on every corner.

● Bostonians are passionate sports fans, enjoying everything from baseball to football, hockey and basketball.

● The city's residents love music (which ranges from local bands to symphony orchestras).

GETTING YOUR BEARINGS

Boston Common and the Public Garden lie at the heart of Boston. To their north is the old residential area of Beacon Hill. Southeast of the Common are the Theater District and Chinatown. The Freedom Trail, which starts on the Common, runs northeast through Old Boston, past Faneuil Hall to the Italian North End. Across the Charles River lies Harvard Square in Cambridge.

A Short Stay in Boston

DAY 1

Morning Start your morning off with a free guided tour of the gorgeous gold-domed State House (▷ 35) to learn about the Sacred Cod and other fun Massachusetts facts.

Mid-morning Make your way to **Faneuil Hall and Marketplace** (▷ 26–27) perusing the artist carts and watching the buskers along the way. Don't forget to go inside Faneuil Hall where many significant and historic speeches have been made. Then walk past City Hall on to Tremont Street, and take a right on Beacon Street for a walk over historic **Beacon Hill** (▷ 24–25). Wander down Mount Vernon Street, and take in upscale **Louisburg Square** (▷ 24–25) and quaint, cobbled Acorn Street.

Lunch At the bottom of the hill, take a right on **Charles Street** (▷ 42). Stop at **Artù** (▷ 45) at 89 Charles Street for a panini, salad or pizza.

Afternoon Visit the antiques shops on Charles Street or visit **Nichols House** (▷ 39) or the **Museum of African American History** (▷ 39).

Mid-afternoon Continue to the end of Charles Street, past the T station to **The Liberty Hotel** (▷ 112) for a drink in the Liberty Lobby bar, and to admire the stunning architectural transformation of this former city jail.

Dinner Return to Charles Street for dinner at the **Beacon Hill Bistro** (▷ 45) or at the nearby **Hungry I** (▷ 45) for a romantic meal with French cuisine.

Evening Take a 10-minute walk through **Boston Common** or the **Public Garden** (▷ 50), or a five-minute taxi ride around it, to the Theater District, to see a play in any of the city's excellent theaters.

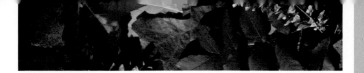

DAY 2

Morning Begin the day at the **Museum of Fine Arts** (▷ 70–71), grabbing a coffee and pastry at one of the several on-site eateries. It's easy to spend a day among its vast collections of French Impressionists, Egyptian artifacts and Early American decorative arts.

Mid-morning Walk along the Fens to the **Isabella Stewart Gardner Museum** (▷ 69) for a look at the home of a Boston legend and a stroll through her fabulous art collection. Stewart was quite a character. She stipulated in her will that the building and everything in it was to stay exactly as she left it, so visitors would enjoy it exactly as she wanted.

Lunch Take the T to Harvard Square for lunch at **Russell House Tavern** (▷ 98), a cozy pub offering American fare.

Afternoon Cross Harvard Yard to see the one-of-a-kind collection of glass flowers at the **Harvard Museum of Natural History** and a look at the Native American collections at the adjoining **Peabody Museum** (▷ 89).

Mid-afternoon Take a break from museums at **L.A. Burdick Chocolate** (▷ 98) before continuing down Brattle Street for a look at the **Longfellow House** (▷ 92).

Dinner Choose between two of Cambridge's most sophisticated restaurants. Chef Jason Bond's **Bondir** (▷ 97) is tiny, but his modern New England dishes are a revelation. Or head for **Oleana** (▷ 98), where chef Ana Sortun focuses on subtly spiced Eastern Mediterranean food: bay scallops with orange-saffron broth, crispy duck with Persian black-eyed peas. Otherwise, dine at **Henrietta's Table** (▷ 98), and enjoy delicious farm-to-table and seasonal local ingredients.

▶ ▶ ▶

ESSENTIAL BOSTON TOP 25

Beacon Hill and Louis-burg Square ▷ 24–25
Elegant residential district with some historic homes.

Boston Common and Public Garden ▷ 50
Open-air playgrounds, ponds and gardens.

Boston Harbor Islands ▷ 102 Unspoiled havens of wildlife, historic forts and beaches.

USS Constitution and Navy Yard ▷ 36–37
Naval museums, historic warships and Bunker Hill.

Trinity Church and Copley Square ▷ 76–77
New (John Hancock Tower) and old (Trinity Church) architecture rub shoulders in this square.

State House ▷ 35
The gold-domed landmark center of state government.

The South End ▷ 74–75
Lively, residential area with great eateries and shops.

Prudential Center and Skywalk ▷ 73
An upscale shopping mall and stunning panoramic views.

Paul Revere House ▷ 34 The legendary revolutionary's North End home and a rare colonial house.

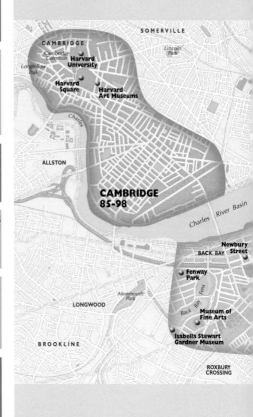

Old State House ▷ 32–33 Best museum for an overview of Boston's rich history.

North End and Old North Church ▷ 30–31
Historic church in the heart of Little Italy.

Newbury Street ▷ 72
Fun shops, luxury boutiques, pavement cafés and trendy restaurants.

These pages are a quick guide to the Top 25, which are described in more detail later. Here they are listed alphabetically, and the tinted background shows which area they are in.

◄ ◄ ◄

Shopping

Every neighborhood in Boston offers something a little different for shoppers. Beacon Hill has boutiques and antiques, while the South End is famous for art. Downtown Crossing offers retail shops galore and Harvard Square is rich with bookshops. In the Back Bay, Newbury Street is famous for its boutiques in lovely 19th-century brownstone buildings. People travel long distances to shop for clothes, from top designer labels to the quirky, here.

Antiques
Like all of New England, Boston is good hunting ground for antiques. Clustered in and around Charles Street, at the foot of Beacon Hill, are dozens of shops. Most of the stores here are specialists, selling oriental rugs, furniture, porcelain, silver or antique maps for serious money. Even if you can't afford to buy, it's a pleasure to browse. In Cambridge, hundreds of dealers in two large markets offer less expensive collectibles, alongside furniture, silverware and other antiques.

Books
Boston has a plethora of bookshops selling new, used and antiquarian titles. Head to the area around Harvard Square for the best range of stores. Whether you're looking for a coffee-table book on Boston to take back home, or something rare, you can browse undisturbed until 11pm in some stores.

ONLY IN BOSTON
Baked beans were invented in Boston by early colonists, who cooked them in molasses. Today, red Boston beans (albeit in candy form) are sold on souvenir stands. The lobster shows up in the usual touristy guises, from fridge magnets to pencil tops and notebooks. As for T-shirts, sweatshirts and baseball caps, they bear logos of local universities, such as Harvard, and local pro teams, including the Patriots, the Bruins, the Celtics and, of course, the 2004, 2007 and 2013 World Series winners, the Red Sox.

Clockwise from top left: Downtown Crossing; colorful handmade glass; shop sign; Harvard Book

Boutiques
Many of the small independent stores in Back Bay, Beacon Hill, the South End and Cambridge brim with interesting finds—from pottery made by Boston artists and soaps created by local beauty companies to hand-knit sweaters. Even on Newbury Street, which at first glance seems to be full of pricey international brands, you'll find local businesses tucked in between.

Outlet Shopping
A massive housing, office and restaurant development in the suburb of Somerville revolves around the outlets at Assembly Row (▷ 95). Only minutes from Downtown on the T are 50 outlet stores, offering discounts of up to 65 percent on clothing, shoes and more.

Farmers' Markets
At the farmers' markets that start up in spring in Copley Square (Tuesday, Friday), South Station (Tuesday, Thursday) and Harvard Square (Tuesday), you can find all the goodies available at roadside farm stands around rural areas of New England—fresh fruits, ice cream, maple syrup, cheese and honey, among other things. The Boston Public Market, a year-round indoor market near Haymarket, is also a great place to shop.

Contemporary Crafts
The best (and easy-to-find) places to shop for contemporary crafts are on Newbury and Charles streets, as well as in Cambridge and the South End.

Store; Faneuil Hall Marketplace; shop sign in Beacon Hill

UNIQUELY BOSTON

Shopping is one of the favorite activities for visitors to Boston, with some tourism surveys ranking its popularity higher than visiting the museums and historic attractions. Clothing costing less than $175 is exempt from the 6.25 percent Massachusetts sales tax. Good shopping areas are located in Back Bay and South End, Beacon Hill and Faneuil Hall, Downtown and Cambridge.

Shopping by Theme

You'll find all sorts of shops in Boston. On this page they are listed by theme with cross references to more detailed information.

Antiques
Cambridge Antique Market (▷ 94)
Charles Street (▷ panel, 42)
Danish Country Antiques (▷ 41)

Books and Maps
Brattle Book Shop (▷ 58)
Eugene Galleries (▷ 41)
Harvard Book Store (▷ 94)
The Harvard Coop (▷ 94)
Out of Town News (▷ 95)
Schoenhof's Foreign Books (▷ 95)
The World's Only Curious George Store (▷ 95)

Children
Boston Children's Museum Shop (▷ 58)
Henry Bear's Park (▷ 95)
Joie de Vivre (▷ 95)
The Red Wagon (▷ 42)
The World's Only Curious George Store (▷ 95)

Clothes and Accessories
Alan Bilzerian (▷ 80)
Coach (▷ 41)
Crush Boutique (▷ 80)
Lucky Brand (▷ 80)
Flock Boutique (▷ 80)
Goorin Bros (▷ 80)
Holiday Boutique (▷ 42)
Life is Good (▷ 80)
Linens on the Hill (▷ 42)
Mint Julep (▷ 95)
St. John Boutique (▷ 58)
The Tannery (▷ 58)
Tess & Carlos (▷ 95)
Vineyard Vines (▷ 81)
Wish Boutique (▷ 42)

Crafts
Bead + Fiber (▷ 80)
Cambridge Artists' Cooperative (▷ 94)

Districts and Malls
Assembly Row (▷ panel, 95)
Barneys New York (▷ 80)
CambridgeSide Galleria (▷ 41)
Charles Street (▷ panel, 42)
Downtown Crossing (▷ 58)
Harvard Square (▷ 94)
Newbury Street (▷ panel, 81)
Prudential Center (▷ 81)

Food
Beacon Hill Chocolates (▷ 41)
Cabot's Candy (▷ 94)
Cardullo's (▷ 94)
Savenor's (▷ 42)

Gifts/Household
Abodeon (▷ 94)
Black Ink (▷ 41)
Boston Pewter Company (▷ 41)
Bostonian Society Museum Shop (▷ 41)
Bromfield Pen Shop (▷ 58)
Flat of the Hill (▷ 42)
Geoclassics (▷ 42)
Gifted (▷ 80)
ICA Store (▷ 58)
Leavitt & Peirce Inc. (▷ 95)
Rugg Road Paper Company (▷ 42)
Simon Pearce (▷ 81)
Shake the Tree (▷ 42)

Music
Newbury Comics (▷ 81)

Outdoor Gear
Allen Edmonds (▷ 80)
Foot Paths (▷ 58)
Modell's Sporting Goods (▷ 81)
The North Face (▷ 81)

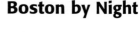

Boston by Night

Entertainment ranges from the Boston Symphony, Boston Ballet and traveling Broadway shows to rock concerts, avant-garde dance and student theater. In summer, see free movies, concerts and theater on outdoor stages.

Illuminations
For magical views of Boston's skyline visit the Prudential Skywalk, or cross over the Charles River to Cambridge on the T. Memorial Drive, between Longfellow and Harvard bridges, which is a good spot to view the floodlit Downtown skyscrapers. In winter, the trees twinkle with festive lights.

People-Watching
One of the best spots for people-watching is North End, where Italian music fills the narrow streets and restaurants hum with the chatter of families. On Newbury Street people sit outdoors in cafés surveying the pedestrian parade.

Clubs and Bars
Head to Lansdowne Street, near Kenmore Square for clubs. For cocktails and to catch the latest music, try Boylston Place, a little alley in the Theater District. The Regattabar (▷ 97) on Harvard Square is one of the best-known jazz venues on the East Coast.

Late-Night Restaurants
Most restaurants do not serve after midnight, but you could try Chinatown, where many places stay open until 4am. In the South End, several restaurants serve until 1am on weekends.

From top: Faneuil Hall; Fenway Park; Chinatown; nightclub; Hatch Shell

LIVE ENTERTAINMENT
There are summer concerts at Hatch Shell (▷ 83), as well as free movies. Look for free band concerts at City Hall Plaza (☎ 617/635-4505) in July and August, and for performances by Boston Landmarks Orchestra (☎ 617/987-2000; landmarksorchestra.org).

Where to Eat

Once known primarily as the home of beans and cod, Boston has blossomed into a first-rate culinary center.

Eclectic Menus
Boston's had a culinary awakening of sorts in recent years, with all sorts of award-winning chefs (including James Beard winners and Top Chef contenders) making their mark in the city. World-class seafood, adventurous diners and creative chefs mean there are lots of great eateries, from food trucks to five-star restaurants.

Bistros
In general, bistros are the most popular genre of restaurant around town; they tend to show up as candlelit spots on Newbury Street or family-run joints in the South End. What they have in common is a sophisticated but unpretentious atmosphere, and often excellent food.

Elegant Dining
A level or two up in price and service, you'll find sophisticated dishes made by Boston's most admired chefs, many of whom have been in the city for years.

Ethnic Restaurants
Boston's ethnic cuisines go beyond Chinatown and the North End Italian neighborhood. In Cambridge, the Portuguese enclave is around Inman Square, and several Irish pubs are nearby. Elsewhere in the city are Ethiopian, Asian and Latin American restaurants.

OPENING TIMES

Restaurant times vary slightly all over the city, but most open for dinner at 5 or 6pm and many serve dinner until 11pm or midnight, and offer an abridged menu if they happen to house a bar. Many of the trendier restaurants do not serve breakfast or lunch, and some are not open at all on Monday. Reservations are a must at any but the most casual places, but particularly at popular eating destinations like Back Bay and the South End.

From top: A Newbury Street café; Faneuil Hall Marketplace; outdoor dining; Chinatown

Where to Eat by Cuisine

There are plenty of places to eat to suit all tastes and budgets in Boston. On this page they are listed by cuisine. For a more detailed description of each venue, see Boston by Area.

American and Mexican
Anthem Kitchen + Bar (▷ 45)
Border Café (▷ 97)
The Butcher Shop (▷ 84)
Café Fleuri (▷ 61)
Craigie on Main (▷ 98)
The Gallows (▷ 84)
Grill 23 & Bar (▷ 61)
Hungry I (▷ 45)
Mr. Bartley's Burger Cottage (▷ 98)
Paramount (▷ 46)

Asian and Middle Eastern
Dumpling Cafe (▷ 61)
Falafel King (▷ 45)
Lala Rokh (▷ 46)
New Shanghai (▷ 62)

Boston's Best
Bondir (▷ 97)
The Bristol Lounge (▷ 61)
Durgin Park (▷ 45)
Marliave (▷ 62)
No. 9 Park (▷ 46)
Oleana (▷ 98)
Park (▷ 98)
Row 34 (▷ 62)
Select Oyster Bar (▷ 84)

Brunch
The Beehive (▷ 84)
Henrietta's Table (▷ 98)

Coffee and Snacks
Caffè Vittoria (▷ 45)
Christina's (▷ 97)
Espresso Love (▷ 61)
Flour Bakery (▷ 84)
Hi-Rise (▷ 98)
L. A. Burdick Chocolate (▷ 98)
Maria's Pastry Shop (▷ 46)

French and Mediterranean
Beacon Hill Bistro (▷ 45)
Bistro du Midi (▷ 61)
Doretta Taverna (▷ 62)
Petit Robert Bistro (▷ 84)
Russel House Tavern (▷ 98)
Teatro (▷ 62)

Italian
Antico Forno (▷ 45)
Artù (▷ 45)
Casa Romero (▷ 84)
La Famiglia Giorgio's Restaurant (▷ 45)
Prezza (▷ 46)

Seafood
Barking Crab (▷ 61)
Legal Sea Foods (▷ 98)
Neptune Oyster (▷ 46)
New Jumbo Seafood (▷ 62)
Rowes Wharf Sea Grille (▷ 62)
Union Oyster House (▷ 46)

Top Tips For…

These great suggestions will help you tailor your ideal visit to Boston, no matter how you want to spend your time. Each sight or listing has a fuller write-up elsewhere in the book.

LAZY MORNINGS
Take a stroll through the Public Garden (▷ 50).
Sip a coffee and people-watch from a table outside Maria's Pastry Shop (▷ 46) in the North End.
Walk along the Charles River Esplanade, the scenic pathway stretching along the river (▷ 78).
Spend time bird-watching at the Mount Auburn Cemetery (▷ 92), a haven for birds.
Take a ferry to the Boston Harbor Islands (▷ 102) for a break from the city.

SPECIALIST SHOPPING
Find the perfect shirt at a Newbury Street boutique (▷ 72).
Get into some of the city's latest music at Newbury Comics (▷ 81).
Act wonderfully childish at The World's Only Curious George Store (▷ 95).
Find one-of-a-kind crafts and handmade jewelry at the ICA Store (▷ 58).
Discover new specialty cheeses and meats at Savenor's Market (▷ 42).
Pick up a unique antique on Charles Street, which is packed with one-of-a-kind shops and galleries.

BOSTON CULTURE
At Isabella Stewart Gardner Museum (▷ 69) see the stunning collection of international art in an attractive mansion.
View world-class collections at the Museum of Fine Arts (▷ 70): European and American art; Egyptian, Chinese and Classical artifacts.
Visit Trinity Church (▷ 76), a classic of Richardson Romanesque.

Clockwise from top left: The swan boats in Boston Public Garden; Boston at night; wildlife in the Public Garden;

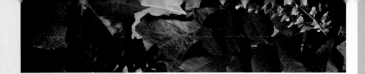

SKYSCRAPERS
Visit the Prudential Tower (▷ 73) and ride up to the 50th-floor Skywalk.
Admire the John Hancock Tower (▷ 77), designed by I.M. Pei & Partners, this glass-enclosed building beautifully reflects those surrounding it.
Ascend Custom House Tower (▷ 38) for the great views from this city landmark and skyscraper-turned-hotel.

COMMUNING WITH NATURE
Relax in the Public Garden (▷ 50), manicured and bustling, it's filled with citydwellers and tourists alike.
Amble through Back Bay Fens (▷ 78). This series of parks and green spaces is part of the Emerald Necklace.
Watch the boats go by in Christopher Columbus Waterfront Park (▷ 38).
Experience the 281 acres (114ha) of lilac blooms, roses and rare Asian trees at Arnold Arboretum (▷ 104) in Jamaica Plain, Boston
Enjoy where nature meets art. The Rose Fitzgerald Kennedy Greenway (▷ 39) offers plenty of places to enjoy public art, bask in nature, or even ride a Boston-themed carousel.

A STATUE TRAIL
See a dramatic ode to the first all-black regiment to fight in the Civil War: Robert Gould Shaw Memorial (▷ 56) facing the State House.
Make Way for the Ducklings: See a charming tribute to Robert McCloskey's children's book, located in the Public Garden (▷ 50).
Honor three great women who contributed to Boston's history—Abigail Adams, Lucy Stone and Phillis Wheatley at the striking Boston Women's Memorial on Commonwealth Avenue (▷ 67).
On your marks: The Tortoise and the Hare statue at Copley Square pays homage to the runners who tackle the Boston Marathon. The finish line is steps away.

Arnold Arboretum; Symphony Hall; Trinity Church reflected in the John Hancock Tower

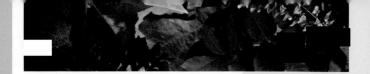

KEEPING THE CHILDREN OCCUPIED

Enjoy a fun, hands-on day of learning at the Museum of Science (▷ 28).

Find interactive exhibits on bubble-making, how televisions work and more at the Boston Children's Museum (▷ 54).

Take a dramatic, spiral trip around a glowing tank full of sea creatures at the New England Aquarium (▷ 53).

Let the kids loose at the Frog Pond Playground at Boston Common (▷ 50). In winter, you can skate on the adjacent pond, while in summer, it turns into a spray park.

ON STAGE

Get in on the act: American Repertory Theater (▷ 96) is Harvard's innovative and ambitious production house.

Watch a highly regarded company performing classical and contemporary productions at José Mateo's Ballet Theatre (▷ 96).

Enjoy dinner and a show at The Beehive (▷ 84) in the South End, which offers an eclectic menu and live music nightly.

LOOKING FOR A BARGAIN

Visit Harvard's three art museums Uniting the Fogg, Busch-Reisinger and Arthur M. Sackler museums is architect Renzo Piano's glass roof (▷ 89).

At the Museum of Fine Arts, pay what you like for entry on Wednesday nights after 4pm (▷ 70).

Find half-price theater tickets the day of a performance at BosTix booths (▷ panel, 59) at Faneuil Hall Marketplace and Copley Square.

ENJOYING NEW ENGLAND SEAFOOD

Head to Legal Sea Foods (▷ 98), a locally based chain known for fresh lobsters and clam chowder.

On the water: Enjoy seafood and views of the water at the Barking Crab (▷ 61).

Pick out your own lobster at New Jumbo Seafood (▷ 62) in Chinatown for a fresh take on seafood.

From top: The Boston Children's Museum; the Museum of Fine Arts, Faneuil Hall; a seafood platter

Boston by Area

BEACON HILL TO CHARLESTOWN

BOSTON COMMON TO THE WATERFRONT

BACK BAY AND THE SOUTH END

CAMBRIDGE

FARTHER AFIELD

This neighborhood merges historic buildings and monuments with skyscrapers.

Beacon Hill to Charlestown

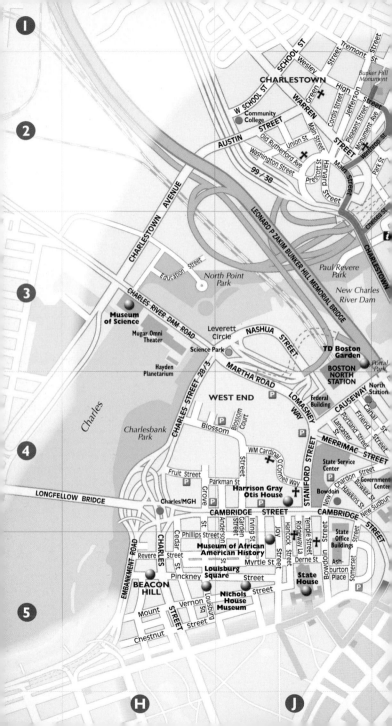

SHEAFE STREET

Lexington St.

Vernon Street

prospect St.

Chestnut Street

Adams St.

Decatur Street

FATHER ADAMSKI MEMORIAL HIGHWAY

2nd Avenue

3rd Avenue

5th Street

6th Street

Lincoln Avenue

8th Street

Chelsea Rd.

Constitution Rd.

Constitution Museum

National Historical Park

Shipyard House

Boston Inner Harbor

USS Constitution
and Charlestown
Navy Yard

Bunker Hill
Pavilion

BRIDGE ST

COMMERCIAL STREET

Charter Street

Copp's Hill Burying Ground

Medford Street

Snowhill Street

Hull Street

Sheafe St.

Salem St.

Old North
Church

Sumner Tunnel (Toll)

Callahan Tunnel

PRINCE STREET

ENDICOTT STREET

NORTH END

N Bennet St.

SALEM STREET

HANOVER STREET

Tileston Street

Bennett Street

Paul Revere Statue

Hanover Ave

Harris St.

Clark St.

ATLANTIC AVENUE

Paul Revere
House

Fleet Street

Lewis Street

Fulton Street

Commercial Street

Eastern Ave

P

P

P

Cross Street

North End Park

Haymarket

CONGRESS STREET

Union Street

New
England
Holocaust
Memorial

James Curley
Statues

P

Christopher Columbus
Waterfront Park

Rose Fitzgerald Kennedy
Greenway

Wharf District Park

New City Hall

Government Center

Samuel Adams
Statue

Faneuil
Marketplace

Corn Hill

State St.

Faneuil
Hall

Chatham St.

Ames
Building

STATE STREET

INDIA ST.

Custom
House
Tower

Old State
House

0   250 m

0   250 yds

K

L

Beacon Hill to Charlestown

Beacon Hill and Louisburg Square

- Louisburg Square
- Pinckney Street and its view of Charles River
- Nichols House Museum
- Charles Street shops and restaurants

Beacon Hill is an enclave of elegant redbrick houses in a leafy maze of steep streets and narrow, cobbled lanes—it is a delightful area to explore on foot.

Wealthy area After the opening of the State House on its southern slope, Beacon Hill was developed as a prestigious residential area by entrepreneurs including Boston's famous architect Charles Bulfinch. Boston's top families swiftly moved in. Rich as they were, these families were also the personification of Puritan reserve. Showiness was taboo, so the houses were restrained, with elegant doorways and ironwork gracing plain brick facades.

Perfectly preserved To soak up the magic of it all, choose a sunny day and just wander, noting

Clockwise from left: Mount Vernon Street; leafy Louisburg Square; cobbled Acorn Street in Beacon Hill; a redbrick building in the Beacon Hill district; fall leaves; De Luca's Market on Charles Street

the pillared porticoes, genteel fanlights and flowery window boxes. A walk through Beacon Hill leads you to some of the city's most treasured corners, including Mount Vernon Street, Chestnut Street, tiny Acorn Street and, best of all, Louisburg Square. Here Bulfinch's lovely bow fronts look onto a central garden reminiscent of a European square. Notice how the street lamps are lighted all day and look for the purple window panes: Manganese oxide in a batch of glass reacted with sunlight to produce discolored but now highly prized panes. To see inside a Beacon Hill home, visit the Nichols House Museum. On the hill's north slope from Pinckney Street down to Cambridge Street, the houses are smaller and more varied. The area has several important sites in the history of Boston's African-American community.

THE BASICS

✚ H5

✉ Bounded by Beacon Street, Embankment Road, Cambridge Street, Bowdoin Street

🍴 Choice in Charles Street

🚇 Park Street, Charles/ MGH, Arlington, Bowdoin (closed Sat)

♿ Steep hills, some uneven surfaces

❓ Historic New England tours of Beacon Hill; Black Heritage Trail: See Museum of African American History (▷ 39)

Faneuil Hall and Marketplace

- Great Hall
- Grasshopper weather-vane on the roof
- Quincy's granite market buildings
- Street entertainers
- Food vendors in Quincy Market
- Anne Whitney's (1880) statue of Samuel Adams in front of Faneuil Hall

Faneuil Hall is a landmark for all Americans, the place where the iniquities of the British government were first debated in the 1770s. Now, its marketplace is a landmark for visitors.

"Cradle of Liberty" A wealthy trader of Huguenot origins, Peter Faneuil presented the town the market hall with a meeting room above. Ever since, the lower hall has been used as a market and the galleried upper hall has been a place for public gatherings. In the 1700s, because the town meetings frequently discussed the problems with Britain that led up to the revolution and independence, Faneuil Hall became known as America's "Cradle of Liberty." Since then national issues, from the abolition of slavery to the Vietnam War, have

Clockwise from left: The exterior of Faneuil Hall, a market stall at Faneuil Hall Market Place, the bustling interior of Quincy's marketplace, the grand exterior of Quincy market

been aired here. The room bears all the trademarks of Charles Bulfinch, the architect who built so much of Boston. He expanded the hall in 1805. Inside Faneuil Hall, visitors will find park rangers, ready to offer tours and advice.

Quincy's marketplace Despite the expansion, more space was needed. In 1826, with some inspired town planning that radically changed Boston's waterfront, mayor Josiah Quincy filled in Town Dock and built over the wharves, providing a granite market hall flanked by granite warehouses. These were a wholesale food market until the 1960s after which the area was renovated and revitalized. Today it is still a major tourist attraction (known as Faneuil Hall Marketplace or Quincy Market) with shops, pushcarts, eating places and street entertainers.

THE BASICS

faneuilhallmarketplace.com

🚇 K5

✉ Congress Street

☎ 617/242-5642

🕐 Great Hall: 9–6 (when not in use)

🍴 A plethora of eating places nearby

🚇 State, Aquarium, Government Center

♿ Good

🎫 Great Hall: free

❓ Great Hall: 15-min talk every half hour

Museum of Science

HIGHLIGHTS

● Lightning demo
● Full-motion simulator
● Natural Mysteries
● Mugar Omni Theater shows

TIPS

● Tickets for special exhibits often sell out during school vacation weeks. Buy in advance online.
● Arrive at least a half hour early for Mugar Omni Theater shows to get the best seats.

This place buzzes and hums with excited children running around pressing lots of buttons and peering into things. There are hundreds of interactive exhibits, as well as live presentations.

"It's awesome" Don't miss the dramatic indoor lightning demos in the Theater of Electricity, where the world's largest Van de Graaff generator creates 2.5 million volts of electricity. Between shows, take part in the popular Hands-On Laboratory. Close by, peer into the mouth of a T-Rex. A large portion of the museum has special exhibits, such as the free-flying Butterfly Garden, or cutting-edge 4D films. The Thrill Ride 360, a simulator with full-motion, 360-degree pitch, roll, and spin technology, takes you on a wild roller-coaster

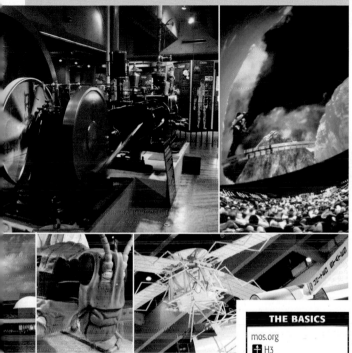

Clockwise from far left: A father and son examine an exhibit at the museum; the blur of the fast-spinning wheels of a steam-powered engine; a crowded show in the Mugar Omni Theater; a model space station; a giant locust model; the museum from the outside reflected in the Charles River

ride or a flight over Boston. Other exhibits include the Natural Mysteries, where you learn about scientific classification. There are also presentations at the Science Live! Stage.

Mugar Omni Theater and the Planetarium

Lie back and be enveloped in the sight and sound of an IMAX movie in the five-story screen of the Mugar Omni Theater. Multimedia presentations at the Charles Hayden Planetarium cover astronomical subjects. Evening laser shows also take place here.

Star struck The museum offers Astronomy After Hours every Friday night (weather permitting) between 8:30 and 10pm at the Gilliland Observatory on the roof allowing you to gaze at the stars, planets and the Moon.

THE BASICS

mos.org

✚ H3

✉ Science Park

☎ 617/723-2500

🕐 Jul 5–Labor Day Sat–Thu 9–7, Fri 9–9. Labor Day– Jul 4 Sat–Thu 9–5, Fri 9–9. Extended hours over school holidays

🍴 Six on premises

🚇 Science Park

♿ Excellent. Sight- and hearing-impaired facilities

💰 Expensive. Separate tickets for Planetarium, Laser Show, Mugar Omni Theater. Combination ticket discounts. Boston CityPass applies

🛍 Good shop

North End and Old North Church

- Paul Revere House
- Old North Church Steeple
- Copp's Hill Burying Ground
- Feast-day processions
- Italian groceries, coffee shops and restaurants

TIP

- The North End explodes with life and color in late August for the Feast of St. Anthony.

The North End is Boston's oldest and most spirited district. This is where the British colonists settled in the 17th century, and now, after various ups and downs, it is a lively Italian quarter.

Little Italy The North End is separated from the rest of Boston by an area that was once a major highway, and is now a park. When the colonists arrived it was also all but cut off, surrounded then by water at the end of a narrow peninsula. The colonists' erratic street plan survives, but the only building from the 17th century is Paul Revere House. Once the elite had moved to Beacon Hill in the early 19th century, the area played host to waves of immigrants, first the Irish, then East Europeans and Portuguese and finally Italians.

From far left: The equestrian statue of Paul Revere with St. Stephen's Church beyond; Old North Church is now overshadowed by office buildings; the decorative sign that welcomes visitors to North End

WELCOME

BOSTON'S HISTORIC NORTH END

NORTH END BUSINESS ALLIANCE

Paul Revere Mall On Hanover Street, opposite St. Stephen's Church, the mall connects the North End's main street to Old North Church. This tree-shaded park is James Rego Square, but locals call it the Prado. Standing at one end is a statue of Paul Revere (▷ panel, 125).

Old North Church It was from Old North that Revere's signal was given to the patriots in Charlestown that the British were on their way to Lexington where, the next day, the first battle of the War of Independence took place.

Copp's Hill Burying Ground Up the hill in front of Old North Church is a former Native American lookout point. In 1659 it became a burying ground, visited now for its rows of slate and stone headstones.

THE BASICS

oldnorth.com
✛ K4/K3
✉ Bounded by Commercial Street and Greenway
🕐 Old North Church, daily. Behind-the-scenes tours: Mar–Dec daily
🍴 Plenty around Hanover and Salem streets
🚇 Haymarket, North Station, Aquarium, State
♿ Some hills and uneven sidewalks

Old State House

HIGHLIGHTS

● Lion and unicorn
● Balcony from which the Declaration of Independence was read
● Exhibit showing topographical changes

TIPS

● Check the website for the latest events program.
● Don't miss the tiny phial of tea leaves saved from the Boston Tea Party.
● Light up the topographical map to see how much of Boston is built on landfill.

This is the city's oldest public building, once the seat of British colonial government. Surrounded by taller—but far less significant—buildings, it seems so tiny now. It holds a first-rate museum.

Colonial capital Built in 1713 to replace an earlier Town House, the Old State House was the British governor's seat of office, home to the judicial court and to the Massachusetts Assembly. The scene of many a confrontation between the colonists and their rulers, it was here that James Otis railed against the "tyranny of taxation without representation" and it was under the balcony at the east end that the "Boston Massacre" took place in 1770: Five colonists were killed in a clash with British soldiers, a key event in the years leading up to the

From far left: The lion and unicorn are clearly visable on the east front of the building; the interior of the Old State House

Revolution. From the same balcony, the Declaration of Independence was read on July 18, 1776, and is still read every July 4. At this point the gilded lion and unicorn on the east front, symbols of the British Crown, were destroyed. From 1780 until 1798, this was the Massachusetts State House. It was used for commercial purposes, gradually falling into disrepair until the Bostonian Society was founded in 1881 to restore it. The lion and the unicorn were returned to their place, balanced now by the American eagle and the Massachusetts seal.

A museum of Boston The building is home to the Bostonian Society's museum, which traces the city's topographical, political, economic and social history, with a fine collection of maritime art and revolutionary memorabilia.

THE BASICS

bostonhistory.org

➕ K5

✉ 206 Washington Street

☎ 617/720-1713

🕐 Jun–Aug daily 9–6; Sep–May 9–5

🍴 Nearby

🚇 State, Government Center, Downtown Crossing

♿ No access

💲 Inexpensive. Boston CityPass applies

🛍 Shop

Paul Revere House

From left to right: The bedroom in Paul Revere House and views of the exterior

THE BASICS

paulreverehouse.org
➕ K4
✉ 19 North Square
☎ 617/523-2338
🕐 Nov to mid-Apr daily 9.30–4.15; mid-Apr to Oct daily 9.30–5.15. Jan–Mar closed Mon
🍴 Nearby
🚇 Government Center, State, Aquarium, Haymarket
♿ Wheelchair access first floor only
💲 Inexpensive
❓ Tours of early Georgian Pierce/Hichborn House

HIGHLIGHTS

● Revere's own account of his ride
● Period furnishings

TIPS

● Avoid the house on spring and fall afternoons, when it is often overrun by groups of schoolchildren.
● Check ahead for the appearances by costumed interpreters.

This house is all that remains of the 17th-century settlement in today's North End. Not only is it Boston's oldest building, it was home to its most celebrated revolutionary, Paul Revere.

The early years The steep-gabled clapboard house that we see today was built in about 1680. Like most houses of the period, it had two rooms on both of its two floors but the positioning of the main staircase at the side of the building, making the rooms larger than normal, was unusual. By 1770, when the silversmith and engraver Paul Revere came to live here, significant alterations had been made, notably the addition of a third floor and a two-story extension at the back. The family lived here during the Revolution, so it was from here that Revere set out on that famous midnight ride (▷ panel, 125). In 1800, after the family sold the house, it became a rooming house, with stores and factory premises on the lower floor. Threatened with demolition in 1902, it was saved by Revere's great-grandson, restored and turned into a museum.

The house today The basic timber skeleton of the house is the original, but the exterior clapboarding, the windows and most of what you see inside are replacements. Go through the kitchen into the living room, furnished in period style. Upstairs, the main bedroom is an elegantly furnished room, which would have doubled as a parlor.

State House

From left to right: The State House exterior and its gleaming gold-leaf dome

Prosperous and newly independent in the late 18th century, Massachusetts needed a larger, more imposing State House. Charles Bulfinch's masterpiece is a landmark in American architecture.

Hub of the Hub Bulfinch began designing the new State House on his return from England, much influenced by Robert Adam's Renaissance style. Construction began in 1795 on a prominent piece of Beacon Hill land. Cut off in your mind's eye the side wings (an early 20th century addition), and focus on Bulfinch's dignified two-story portico and dome. Its original shingles were covered in copper from the foundry of Paul Revere when the roof began to leak, and the gold leaf was added in 1874.

Seat of government Start your tour in the columned Doric Hall. From here pass through the marble Nurses' Hall and note Bela Pratt's memorial to Civil War nurses. The Italian marble floor in the Hall of Flags was laid by immigrants from Italy. Featured in the stained-glass skylight are the seals of the original 13 states. Up the staircase is the House of Representatives chamber. Here, the Sacred Cod, a symbol of the importance of the fishing industry and a lucky mascot, must hang whenever the 160 state representatives are in session. The dignified barrel-vaulted and Ionic-columned Senate Reception Room is Bulfinch's, as is the Senate Chamber, where 40 senators debate beneath a graceful sunburst dome.

THE BASICS

+ J5
✉ Beacon Street
☎ 617/727-3676
◷ Mon–Fri 10–3.30 (except holiday Mondays)
🍴 None
Ⓟ Park Street
♿ Partial wheelchair access
💵 Free
❓ Regular tours (45 min); last tour 3.30. It is advisable to call in advance to reserve a guided tour

HIGHLIGHTS

● Gold dome (regilded in 1997 with 22-carat gold leaf)
● Sacred Cod
● Senate Reception Room
● Senate Chamber
● JFK statue

TIP

● To enter the State House for tours use the side entrance on Bowdoin Street.

USS *Constitution* and Navy Yard

TOP 25

HIGHLIGHTS

● Museum: details of a sailor's daily diet and duties
● USS *Constitution*: cramped lower deck

TIPS

● If you are walking the Freedom Trail from Boston, get here by 3pm to take a tour of the ship.
● Kids will love the top floor of the museum, where they can fire ships' cannons in interactive games.

"Old Ironsides," as she is commonly called, is the oldest commissioned warship afloat in the world. More than 200 years old, she is moored in the Charlestown Navy Yard.

The Navy Yard From 1800 to 1974 the Charlestown Navy Yard played an important role building, repairing and supplying Navy warships. Its mission now is to interpret the history of naval shipbuilding. Representing the ships built here are USS *Constitution* and the World War II destroyer USS *Cassin Young*, both of which may be boarded. The old granite Building 22 now houses the USS *Constitution* Museum, where objects record the frigate's 200-year career and give a picture of life aboard. Also open is the Commandant's House. The Bunker

Clockwise from far left: Gleaming cannons on the restored frigate USS Constitution, "Old Ironsides"; the world's oldest commissioned floating battleship, at dock in Charlestown Navy Yard; detail of the craftsmanship and rigging that have kept this venerable vessel afloat; view of the prow and masts; rigging winch

Hill Pavilion's diorama, "The Battle of Bunker Hill," tells the story of this battle. The Bunker Hill Monument stands atop the hill. It is visible from, and is within walking distance of, the Navy Yard. Climb its 294 steps for good views.

USS *Constitution* The highlight of the Yard is "Old Ironsides." Launched in Boston in 1797, she is still part of the US Navy, whose sailors lead tours round the cramped quarters. Vulnerable though the wooden sides seem now, it was her tough live-oak frames that enabled her to survive the War of 1812 undefeated and win her nickname. After surviving three wars, the vessel was frail and needed to be heavily reconstructed. She takes a turn in Boston Harbor every July 4, so that the side that faces the elements can be changed.

THE BASICS

history.navy.mil/ ussconstitution

nps.gov/bost

🚩 K2

✉ Charlestown Navy Yard

☎ Navy Yard Visitor Center: 617/242-5601

🕐 USS *Constitution* Museum: Apr–Oct 9–6; Nov–Mar 10–5. USS *Constitution*: Apr–Sep Tue–Sun 10–6; Oct Tue–Sun 10–4; Nov–Mar Thu–Sat 10–4. USS *Cassin Young*: Jul, Aug 10–5, Apr–Jun, Sep–Nov 10–4. Closed Dec–Mar. Bunker Hill Monument: daily 9–4.30 (till 5.30 Jul–Aug). Bunker Hill Museum: daily 9–5 (till 6 Jul–Aug)

🍴 In the Navy Yard

Ⓒ North Station or Community College, then 15-min walk

🚤 MBTA Water Shuttle from Long Wharf

♿ All wheelchair accessible except USS *Cassin Young*

✋ All free except USS *Constitution* Museum (donation). 18s and over need photo ID

More to See

AMES BUILDING

ameshotel.com

The 14-floor, 1893 Ames Building is considered to be Boston's first skyscraper and is now an elegant boutique hotel (▷ 110).

🔢 K5 ✉ 1 Court Street 🚇 State

CHRISTOPHER COLUMBUS WATERFRONT PARK

This is a small waterfront park near Faneuil Hall Marketplace and North End. Sit under the trellis or on the grass with a picnic and watch the boats sail by.

🔢 L4 ✉ Atlantic Avenue 🚇 Aquarium
🕐 Daily 🖐 Free

CUSTOM HOUSE TOWER

The 30-floor clock tower, built in 1915, is a Boston landmark and was for a long time the city's tallest building. At street level you see how odd it looks stuck on the roof of the original Custom House, built in 1847 in Greek Revival style, at what was then the water's edge. It is now a hotel, but the public can go up to the 26th floor, open-air observatory to enjoy the amazing views over the city.

🔢 K5 ✉ 3 McKinley Square
🕐 Observatory: call for hours (617/310-6300, marriott.com) 🚇 State, Aquarium

HARRISON GRAY OTIS HOUSE

historicnewengland.org

Once home to one of the leading lights in post-Revolutionary Boston politics Harrison Gray Otis (1765–1844) this is a fine example of Federal-style architecture (1780–1830). Otis and his wife, Sally, were lavish entertainers and the parlor, dining room and drawing room, provide an insight into social manners of the day, while bedrooms, kitchens and servant quarters give you a glimpse of family life. One room shows the mansion as it looked when it was a boarding house.

🔢 J4 ✉ 141 Cambridge Street ☎ 617/994-5920 🕐 Wed–Sun 11–5. Tours on the hour and half hour 🍴 None 🚇 Bowdoin (closed weekends), Charles/MGH, Government

Commercial Wharf adjacent to Christopher Columbus Park on the waterfront

The Custom House Tower at night

Center 🚫 Wheelchairs first floor only
🅿 Moderate. Historic New England
members free ❓ Walking tours of Beacon
Hill mid-May to mid-Oct, Sat (call ahead for
bookings). Shop

MUSEUM OF AFRICAN AMERICAN HISTORY

maah.org

A museum dedicated to the history
of African-Americans in Boston is
housed in the 1806 African
Meeting House. Once a center for
social and political activity, it is now
a focal point on the Black Heritage
Trail, a 1.6-mile (2.5km) guided or
self-guided walking tour of pre-Civil
War Beacon Hill sites, including the
Abiel Smith School and the Robert
Gould Shaw Monument.

➕ J5 ✉ 46 Joy Street ☎ 617/725-0022
🕐 Mon–Sat 10–4 🚇 Charles/MGH, Park
Street, Government Center 🅿 Inexpensive

NEW ENGLAND HOLOCAUST MEMORIAL

nehm.org

Six tall glass towers, the work of
Stanley Saitowitz (1995), rise 54
feet in the air. Etched numerals rep-
resent the Holocaust's six million
victims. The memorial is especially
poignant after dark, when floodlit.

➕ K4 ✉ Union Street 🕐 Daily 🚇 State

NICHOLS HOUSE MUSEUM

nicholshousemuseum.org

One of Boston's earliest Federal-
style houses, this elegant four-floor
Beacon Hill house was built by
Charles Bulfinch in 1804 and is
furnished with Nichols family art
and antiques.

➕ J5 ✉ 55 Mount Vernon Street
☎ 617/227-6993 🕐 Apr–Oct Tue–Sat

11–4; Nov–Mar Thu–Sat 11–4. By tour
only; last tour starts at 4pm 🚇 Park Street
🅿 Moderate

ROSE FITZGERALD KENNEDY GREENWAY

rosekennedygreenway.org

The Rose Kennedy Greenway, a
gorgeous replacement to a former
aboveground highway and eyesore,
is a 1.5-mile (2.4km) stretch of
parks, filled with public art, spray
fountains, a carousel, food trucks
and the site of many festival and
events. It's a lovely place to rest,
people-watch and take in the city.

➕ L5 ✉ Atlantic Avenue ☎ 617/621-
3001 🕐 Daily, 7am 11pm 🚇 Haymarket,
Aquarium, Chinatown, South Station 🅿 Free

TD BOSTON GARDEN

tdgarden.com

The "Garden," is the home of the
Celtics (basketball) and Bruins (ice
hockey). Concerts and other events
are also held there.

➕ J3 ✉ 100 Legends Way ☎ Ticketmaster:
800/745-3000 🚇 North Station

Museum of African American History

Freedom Trail

This walk follows a section of the red-bricked (see above) Freedom Trail which links sites from Boston's Colonial and revolutionary era.

DISTANCE: 1.5 miles (2.4km) **ALLOW:** 1–4 hours

START

BOSTON COMMON (▷ 50)
🚩 J5 🚇 Park Street

END

COPP'S HILL (▷ 31)
🚩 K3 🚇 North Station

❶ From the information center on Boston Common head for the State House (▷ 35). Walk down Park Street to "Brimstone Corner" where gunpowder was stored.

❽ Back in Hanover Street, turn onto Revere Mall, passing Paul Revere's statue (▷ 31), with the Old North Church (▷ 31) steeple ahead. Continue uphill to Copp's Hill.

❷ On Tremont Street, in the Granary Burying Ground, find the graves of many famous people. King's Chapel (▷ 55) is the oldest church site in Boston still in use.

❼ Cross Blackstone Street and cross the Rose Fitzgerald Kennedy Greenway (▷ 39) to the North End. Turn onto Richmond Street to reach North Square and Paul Revere House (▷ 34).

❸ On School Street a sidewalk mosaic marks the site of the first free school, open to all. Pass the statue of Benjamin Franklin.

❻ The trail continues between the New England Holocaust Memorial (▷ 39) and the Union Oyster House (▷ 46) to Hanover Street.

❹ Diagonally right, past the Irish Famine Memorial (▷ 55), is Old South Meeting House (▷ 56), where the Boston Tea Party started. Follow the red line along Washington Street to Old State House (▷ 32–33).

❺ Cross onto Congress Street to get to Faneuil Hall (▷ 26–27).

Shopping

BEACON HILL CHOCOLATES

beaconhillchocolates.com

Fine chocolate is transformed into delectable and beautiful gifts and packaged in elegant boxes. The tiny shop's entrance is just around the corner from Charles Street.

⊞ H5 ⊠ 91 Charles Street ☎ 617/725-1900 🚇 Charles/MGH

BLACK INK

blackinkboston.squarespace.com

This shop features an eclectic selection of gifts and novelties, such as shark staplers, alphabet cookie cutters and bright green frog banks.

⊞ H5 ⊠ 101 Charles Street ☎ 617/723-3883 🚇 Charles/MGH, Arlington

BOSTON PEWTER COMPANY

bostonpewtercompany.com

All manner of traditional, handcrafted pewter items fill shelves here, including pieces for the home (lighting, sculpture and dishes) and giftware.

⊞ K5 ⊠ South Market, Faneuil Hall Marketplace ☎ 617/523-1776 🚇 State, Government Center

BOSTONIAN SOCIETY MUSEUM SHOP

bostonhistory.org

Buy a little piece of New England history from this store, created to support Boston's Historical Society. The group sells books about New England's past, plus quilts, teas, mugs and prints.

⊞ K5 ⊠ South Canopy, Faneuil Hall Marketplace ☎ 617/742-4744 🚇 State, Government Center

CAMBRIDGESIDE GALLERIA

cambridgesidegalleria.com

More than 120 stores and restaurants including Gap, Sears, Macy's, Best Buy, California Pizza Kitchen and the Cheesecake Factory can be found here, ideal if you need some retail therapy.

⊞ G3 ⊠ 100 CambridgeSide Place ☎ 617/621-8666 🚇 Lechmere

COACH

coach.com

This popular and high-quality international leather goods company sells an impressive selection of handbags, shoes and other accessories.

⊞ K5 ⊠ South Market, Faneuil Hall Marketplace ☎ 617/723-1777 🚇 State, Government Center

DANISH COUNTRY ANTIQUES

danishcountry.net/

True to its name, this gem full of imported finds sells well-preserved, rustic pieces from Denmark. Don't miss the fine selection of tables—for the kitchen, dining room or living room

⊞ H4 ⊠ 138 Charles Street ☎ 617/227-1804 🚇 Charles/MGH

EUGENE GALLERIES

eugenegalleries.com

An interesting gallery specializing in old maps and prints, with a good selection covering Boston. This is the place to discover heirlooms and excellent gifts.

⊞ H5 ⊠ 76 Charles Street ☎ 617/227-3062 🚇 Charles/MGH

THE CHAIN

Most of the major American clothes chains are represented in the city: Abercrombie & Fitch (Faneuil Hall Marketplace), Banana Republic (CambridgeSide Galleria, Newbury Street), Giorgio Armani (Newbury Street), Saks Fifth Avenue, Ann Taylor, Lacoste, Lord & Taylor, Gucci, Vera Bradley and Kate Spade (Prudential Center).

FLAT OF THE HILL

flatofthehill.com

This charming gift boutique is crammed with garden accessories, hand-knit throws, pretty stationery and more.

✚ H5 ✉ 60 Charles Street ☎ 617/619-9977
🚇 Charles/MGH

GEOCLASSICS

geoclassics.com

A store selling beautiful geological wonders that have been transformed into fine jewelry—perfect for gifts.

✚ K5 ✉ 7 North Market, Faneuil Hall Marketplace ☎ 617/523-6112 🚇 Government Center, State

HOLIDAY BOUTIQUE

holidayboutique.net

Bold and modern women's fashions line the racks of this small but well-stocked shop. As well as in-house Holiday creations, find one-of-a-kind designs by Eva Franco, Ecru, David Lerner, J Brand and Kirribilla.

✚ H5 ✉ 53 Charles Street ☎ 617/973-9730
🚇 Charles/MGH

LINENS ON THE HILL

linensonthehill.com

This is the perfect place to pick up fine French linens: sheets, pillowcases, tablecloths, nightgowns and robes. The store also stocks quality homeware.

✚ H6 ✉ 52 Charles Street ☎ 617/227-1255
🚇 Charles/MGH, Arlington

THE RED WAGON

theredwagon.com

An independent shop featuring bright, creatively casual T-shirt sets, dresses, knitwear and more for babies and young children.

✚ H5 ✉ 69 Charles Street ☎ 617/524-9402
🚇 Charles/MGH

RUGG ROAD PAPER COMPANY

ruggroadpaper.com

Gorgeous handmade papers and stationery are the stock-in-trade at this lovely shop, which also offers beautiful cards, journals and gift wrap.

✚ H5 ✉ 105 Charles Street ☎ 617/742-0002
🚇 Charles/MGH

SAVENOR'S

savenorsmarket.com

The late culinary queen Julia Child used to order her meats from this specialty market, where you'll find everything from giraffe meat to wild mushrooms.

✚ H5 ✉ 160 Charles Street ☎ 617/723-6328
🚇 Charles/MGH

SHAKE THE TREE

shakethetreeboston.com

Filled with a quirky assortment of everything from clothing to books, this shop is a delight to wander and a great place to pick up gifts.

✚ K4 ✉ 67 Salem Street, North End
☎ 617/742-0484 🚇 Haymarket

WISH BOUTIQUE

wishboston.com

A colorful women's clothing store, with great dresses by Nanette Lepore, Rebecca Taylor and Theory.

✚ H5 ✉ 49 Charles Street ☎ 617/227-4441
🚇 Charles/MGH

CHARLES STREET

This is a delightful street of stores and restaurants, running north from the Public Garden through the flat area of Beacon Hill. It specializes in (mostly pricey) antiques shops but has several gift shops and galleries, too, and a selection of places where you can get a bite to eat.

✚ J4 🚇 Arlington, Charles

Entertainment and Nightlife

21ST AMENDMENT

21stboston.com

Across from the State House, this is a good spot to refuel with beer and specialty sandwiches while walking the Freedom Trail. At night, it attracts a fashionable local crowd.

🔹 J5 ✉ 150 Bowdoin Street ☎ 617/227-7100 🚇 Bowdoin, Park Street

BEACON HILL PUB

A good old-fashioned neighborhood pub favored by students as well as locals for its inexpensive drinks, darts and a jukebox. It serves no food and boasts no frills.

🔹 H5 ✉ 149 Charles Street ☎ 617/625-7100 🚇 Charles/MGH

CHEERS

cheersboston.org

After standing in line for hours, tourists are often disappointed that the inside of the Bull & Finch on Beacon Hill, which served as the model for the television show Cheers, looks nothing like it does on TV. Instead, go to the new Cheers bar in Faneuil Hall, which was designed to be an exact replica of the set.

🔹 K5 ✉ 84 Beacon Street/Faneuil Hall Marketplace ☎ 617/227-9605 or 617/227-0150 🚇 Charles/MGH, Arlington, Haymarket

HONG KONG AT FANEUIL HALL

hongkongboston.com

Two words: scorpion bowls! The booze-filled punch packs a wallop, and fuels a fun but cheesy dance scene.

🔹 K5 ✉ 65 Chatham Street ☎ 617/227-2226 🚇 State

IMPROV ASYLUM

improvasylum.com

Improv Asylum features sketch and improvisational comedy at a North End cabaret-style theater. Make sure you book your tickets in advance.

🔹 K4 ✉ 216 Hanover Street ☎ 617/263-6887 🕐 Shows Tue–Sun 🚇 Haymarket

LAST HURRAH

omnihotels.com

Black-and-white photos from Boston's Golden Age line the walls in the Parker House's upscale hotel bar. The clientele is a mix of hotel guests and politicos.

🔹 K5 ✉ 60 School Street ☎ 617/227-8600 🚇 Government Center, State

SEVENS

Often referred to as the "real Cheers," (of TV fame) this Charles Street institution draws people from all walks of life to drink frosty ones at wooden booths.

🔹 H5 ✉ 77 Charles Street ☎ 617/523-9074 🚇 Charles/MGH

WARREN TAVERN

warrentavern.com

Open since 1780, this is arguably America's most historic watering hole. The pub is named for Doctor Warren, the patriot who ordered Paul Revere and William Dawes to ride to Lexington on the evening of April 18, 1775.

🔹 J2 ✉ 2 Pleasant Street, Charlestown ☎ 617/241-8142 🚇 Community College

NIGHTLIFE AND CRUISES

The *Odyssey* operates evening cruises on a 600-passenger yacht, plus a Sunday jazz brunch and weekday lunches (reservations required). ✉ Rowes Wharf ☎ 617/654-9710 or 866/307-2469; odysseycruises.com. *The Spirit of Boston* has DJs and shows on its dinner-dance cruises. ✉ World Trade Center ☎ 617/748-1450; spiritcruises.com 🕐 Lunch and dinner cruises daily Jun–Oct. Call for the winter schedule

Where to Eat

PRICES	
Prices are approximate, based on a 3-course meal for one person.	
$$$	over $40
$$	$20–$40
$	under $20

ANTHEM KITCHEN + BAR ($$)

anthem-boston.com

Offering a comfortable retreat in bustling Faneuil Hall, Anthem features creative American fare, with lots of lobster dishes, pizzas and burgers.

🚇 K5 ✉ South Market Building, Faneuil Hall ☎ 617/720-5570 🕐 Lunch, dinner daily, Sat & Sun brunch 🚇 State, Government Center

ANTICO FORNO ($)

anticofornoboston.com

Classic Neapolitan pizzas cooked in a brick oven, as well as tasty antipasti and homemade pastas, makes this a perennial North End favorite.

🚇 K4 ✉ 93 Salem Street ☎ 617/723-6733 🕐 Lunch, dinner daily 🚇 Haymarket

ARTÙ ($$)

artuboston.com

Country-style Italian cooking and friendly staff are the hallmarks at this comfortable restaurant. There is a second branch at 89 Charles Street.

🚇 K4 ✉ 6 Prince Street, North End ☎ 617/742-4336 🕐 Lunch, dinner daily 🚇 Haymarket

BEACON HILL BISTRO ($$)

beaconhillhotel.com

This cozy bistro offers fresh and stylish New England fare, with a focus on local ingredients and "shareability."

🚇 H5 ✉ 25 Charles Street ☎ 617/723-7575 🕐 Breakfast, lunch, dinner daily 🚇 Charles/MGH

CAFFÈ VITTORIA ($)

caffevittoria.com

It's easy to feel like you're in Italy at this four-story cafe, which serves up pastries, coffees and boasts a huge grappa menu.

🚇 K4 ✉ 296 Hanover Street ☎ 617/227-7606 🕐 Daily 7am–midnight 🚇 Haymarket

DURGIN PARK ($$)

durgin-park.com

"Established before you were born," is the proud motto here, where hearty New England dishes are served up with an attitude.

🚇 K5 ✉ Faneuil Hall Marketplace ☎ 617/227-2038 🕐 Daily 11.30–10 🚇 State, Aquarium, Government Center

FALAFEL KING ($)

falafelkingofboston.com

For a quick meal, at a reasonable price, Falafel King can't be beat with its tasty and filling kebabs, falafel and shawarma.

🚇 K5 ✉ 260 Washington Street, Downtown Crossing ☎ 617/227-6400 🕐 Mon–Fri 11–6; Sat 11–3.30 🚇 Downtown Crossing, State

LA FAMIGLIA GIORGIO'S RESTAURANT ($$)

lafamigliagiorgios.com

All the favorites, in generous portions, are served at this family-friendly Roman-style restaurant. Diners almost always have leftovers to take home

🚇 K4 ✉ 112 Salem Street ☎ 617/367-6711 🕐 Lunch and dinner daily 🚇 Haymarket

HUNGRY I ($$$)

hungryi.com

Always listed as one of Boston's most romantic restaurant, the Hungry I offers French cuisine in an intimate setting.

🚇 H5 ✉ 71 Charles Street ☎ 617/227-3524 🕐 Lunch Thu–Fri; dinner daily; brunch Sun 🚇 Charles/MGH

LALA ROKH ($$)

lalarokh.com

Refined Persian cuisine is featured at this elegant restaurant. Specialties include chicken with rose petals, cumin and cinnamon. The saffron ice cream is a must-try.

🔢 H5 ✉ 97 Mount Vernon Street ☎ 617/720-5511 🕙 Dinner daily 🚇 Charles/ MGH

MARIA'S PASTRY SHOP ($)

mariaspastry.com

From creating award-winning cannoli and chocolate torrone to tiramisu and Italian cheesecake, the Merola family ensure that Maria's is all about the sweet things in life.

🔢 K4 ✉ 46 Cross Street, North End ☎ 617/523-1196 🕙 Daily 7–7, Sun 7–5 🚇 Haymarket

NEPTUNE OYSTER ($$)

neptuneoyster.com

New Englanders are justly proud of their seafood, and this raw bar serves the freshest and best: Wellfleet clams, little-necks and cherrystones. Carry on with chowders, whole roasted fish and lobster clambake.

🔢 K4 ✉ 63 Salem Street, North End ☎ 617/742-3474 🕙 Daily 11.30–9.30, weekends till 10.30 🚇 State, Government Center

NO. 9 PARK ($$$)

no9park.com

Award-winning chef Barbara Lynch serves French and Italian-inspired dishes at her flagship restaurant on Beacon Hill. The setting is serene and sophisticated and diners in the know order the pre fixe menu and put themselves in Lynch's capable hands.

🔢 J5 ✉ 9 Park Street ☎ 617/742-9991 🕙 Dinner daily 🚇 Park Street

PARAMOUNT ($$)

paramountboston.com

A neighborhood favorite for decades, this family restaurant offers a warm welcome, comfort food and a friendly atmosphere. A good choice if dining with kids.

🔢 H5 ✉ 44 Charles Street ☎ 617/720-1152 🕙 Daily 7am–10pm, 8am–11pm weekends 🚇 Charles/MGH

PREZZA ($$$)

prezza.com

Named for the tiny town the owner's grandmother came from in Italy, Prezza offers classic Italian fare, with a focus on fresh, local ingredients. The wine list is outstanding.

🔢 L4 ✉ 24 Fleet Street, North End ☎ 617/227-1577 🕙 Dinner daily 🚇 Haymarket

UNION OYSTER HOUSE ($$)

unionoysterhouse.com

Regarded more as an historic landmark than an eatery, Union Oyster House has been open since 1826, and has hosted everyone from John F. Kennedy to Leonardo DiCaprio. Take a seat at the oyster bar and enjoy the longtime staff's stories, as well as the raw oysters they're shucking.

🔢 K4 ✉ 41 Union Street ☎ 617/227-2750 🕙 Lunch, dinner daily 🚇 Haymarket

---

NEW ENGLAND DISHES

Try these: lobster, clam chowder, scrod, quahog (a large clam, pronounced "ko hog"), Boston baked beans (slow-cooked for flavor in an earthenware pot), Boston cream pie (chocolate-covered and custard-filled white cake) and Indian pudding (cornmeal, milk and molasses, cooked long and slow).

The bustling area running from Boston Common and the Public Garden to the Waterfront takes you through the Theater District, Chinatown and the Financial District.

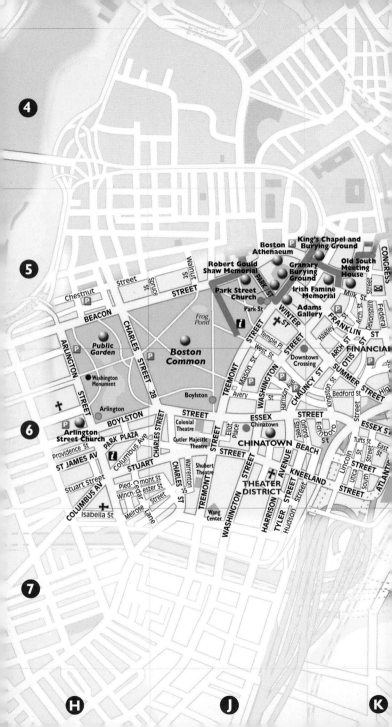

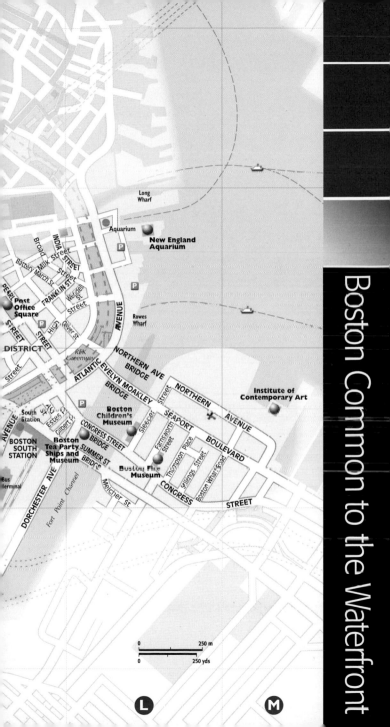

Long
Wharf

Aquarium

**New England
Aquarium**

INDIA STREET

Broad
Battery   Milk
March St.   Street

FRANKLIN ST.

Wendell
St.
Street

PEARL

**Post
Office
Square**

HIGH

STREET

DISTRICT

Street

RFK
Greenway

Rowes
Wharf

AVENUE

NORTHERN AVE.
BRIDGE

ATLANTIC

EVELYN MOAKLEY
BRIDGE

Sleeper   Street

NORTHERN

**Institute of
Contemporary Art**

AVENUE

SEAPORT

South
Station

Estes   St.
Gilbert

CONGRESS STREET
BRIDGE

**Boston
Children's
Museum**

Farnsworth   Street

Thompson Place

BOULEVARD

Boston Wharf Road

Stillings Street

**BOSTON
SOUTH
STATION**

**Boston
Tea Party
Ships and
Museum**

SUMMER ST.
BRIDGE

**Boston Fire
Museum**

CONGRESS

STREET

AVENUE

Bus
Terminal

DORCHESTER AVE.

Fort Point Channel

Melcher St.

0   250 m

0   250 yds

L   M

Boston Common and Public Garden

TOP 25

Pedal-powered Swan Boats, which date from 1877, transport visitors around the lagoon

THE BASICS

J5/H5
Bounded by Beacon, Park, Tremont, Boylston, Arlington streets
Swan Boats: 617/522-1966. Ice-skating: 617/635-2120
Public Garden: daily dawn–10pm. Swan Boats: Apr–Sep. Ice-skating: Dec–Mar
Nearby
Park Street, Boylston, Arlington
Garden and Common free. Swan Boats, skating inexpensive

TIPS

- The Common's Parkman Bandstand frequently features free concerts and plays.
- Try to avoid bringing a car into Central Boston, but if you must, beneath Boston Common is one of the most affordable garages (enter from Charles Street).

Very different in history and character, these adjoining areas of public open space, separated by Charles Street, right in the heart of the city, are held in deep affection. Without them, Boston just wouldn't be Boston.

Boston Common The oldest public park in the US owes its origins to early British settlers who in 1634 acquired the land from a Reverend William Blaxton for common grazing. It was also where criminals were hanged and the dead were buried (in the Central Burying Ground, by Boylston Street). Here, British soldiers camped and George Washington addressed the crowds after Independence. Early in the 1800s paths were laid out and fountains and monuments erected. It is still a place for speeches and demonstrations, but also for street performers and concerts or, in winter, ice-skating at Frog Pond. Although it is safe by day, it's best avoided late at night.

The Public Garden This was created as a botanical garden in 1837. Hundreds of trees were planted and beds, lawns and footpaths were laid out. The garden is perennially beautiful. The focal point is a lagoon, with a little cast-iron suspension bridge. Here, in summer, you can take a ride on the famous Swan Boats. Sculptures include a striking equestrian George Washington (Thomas Ball, 1869) and the Ether Monument, marking the first use of ether as an anaesthetic, here in Boston, in 1846.

Visitors dump parcels of tea over the side of the Boston Tea Party Ship

Boston Tea Party Ships and Museum

Every American child learns about the night of December 16, 1773, when tea was dumped in Boston Harbor. But aboard the *Eleanor* and the *Beaver*, the drama comes to life with actors and visitor participation.

Spirit of '73 Much of what occurred when the Sons of Liberty boarded three ships in Boston Harbor and threw cargo overboard is still blurred by patriotic fervor. Here, you can reconsider the facts and argue the complex whys and wherefores by playing authentic historic roles, reading scripts handed out by staff dressed in period costume. The action-packed one-hour tour gets under way in the replica meeting house, where Sam Adams makes a fiery speech. The arguments for and against revolt are rehearsed. On the two replica ships, moored alongside, everyone gets to "dump the tea" overboard.

Meet the king Among the authentic artifacts in the museum is a 230-year-old "half-chest," one of only two existing tea chests that were thrown in the harbor. Grabbing the attention are holograms, oil paintings of King George III, John Hancock and Lord North that spring into life and carry out a "debate" about the right to impose taxes. An award-winning movie leads you on to the clashes in April, 1775, in Concord and Lexington, just west of Boston. This provides a thought-provoking introduction to the events that led up to the American Revolution.

THE BASICS

bostonteapartyship.com

✠ L6

✉ Congress Street Bridge

☎ 617/338-1773

🕐 Daily 10–5 (4pm off season), tours begin every 30 mins

🍴 Abigail's Tea Room

Ⓣ South Station

♿ Wheelchair access to museum and ship

💲 Expensive; online discount

❓ Annual Boston Tea Party Reenactment, Dec 16

HIGHLIGHTS

● Visitors get involved with the politics
● Meeting the 18th-century characters
● The holograms
● Views of the harbor

TIP

● A great family day out, combined with nearby Boston Children's Museum.

Institute of Contemporary Art

From left: The superb home of the Institute; The Founders' Gallery

THE BASICS

icaboston.org

✚ M6

✉ 100 Northern Avenue

☎ 617/478-3100, Box Office 617/478-3103

🕐 Tue–Wed, Sat–Sun 10–5, Thu–Fri 10–9

🍴 Water Café on site

Ⓢ Courthouse

♿ Wheelchair access

✋ Expensive (free Thu 5–9pm and for families the last Sat of each month, excluding Dec)

❓ Performances, concerts

HIGHLIGHTS

● The architecture
● The interpretation of exhibits
● The outstanding gift shop

TIP

● While in the neighborhood, enjoy lunch or dinner at Row 34 (▷ 62), just a 10-minute walk away, located on Congress Street.

The catalyst for South Boston's revitalized waterfront district was the ICA, set in a dramatic building that hangs out over the water. The building, with its modern art, is right on the HarborWalk that reconnects the city with its roots.

The building The first US work of the architectural firm of Diller Scofidio + Renfro, the dramatic building reaches out over the harbor with a breathtaking cantilevered facade. Its expanses of glass overlook superb views, and the area sheltered by the overhang creates an amphitheater for performances with the water as a backdrop.

The art Superb though the views may be, the building also offers extraordinary opportunities for displaying contemporary art and mounting multi-media presentations. The Institute's permanent collection of 21st-century art includes works by leading names, among them Philip-Lorca diCorcia, Mona Hatoum, Ambreen Butt, Paul Chan, Rineke Dijkstra and Thomas Hirschhorn. The emphasis is on the well-interpreted special exhibitions that explore the complex nature of artistic expression.

HarborWalk This almost continuous 43-mile (69km) linear promenade covers a large portion of Boston's waterfront. The section of HarborWalk that connects Rowe's Wharf to the Institute is worth walking for its own art with beautiful, marine-themed iron sculptures.

TOP 25

New England Aquarium

THE BASICS

neaq.org

🔼 L5

✉ Central Wharf

☎ 617/973-5200

🕐 Jul 1–Labor Day Sun–Thu 9–6, Fri–Sat, holidays 9–7; rest of year Mon–Fri 9–5, Sat, Sun, holidays 9–6

🍴 On premises

Ⓜ Aquarium

♿ Good

💲 Expensive (IMAX is extra). Boston CityPass applies

❓ Concerts, lectures, tours, shop, whale-watching Apr–Oct ☎ 617/973-5200

Immensely popular with families, the Aquarium is home to a four-story coral reef, filled with thousands of Caribbean animals, two touch tanks and several fascinating exhibits.

Penguins, sharks and electric eels In the penguin pool at the base of the Giant Ocean Tank visitors always enjoy the antics of the world's smallest penguin species. At the Shark and Ray Touch Tank, visitors can carefully touch cownose rays, Atlantic rays and epaulette sharks as they swim by, while at the separate Edge of the Sea tidepool touch tank, visitors can pet a sea star or hold a hermit crab.

Exciting exhibits The popular Science of Sharks features shark species from around the world, including a Halmahera walking shark, which uses its fins to crawl. Don't miss the mesmerizing Seajellies exhibit or the Seadragon exhibit, which shine a light on these mysterious sea creatures. The showstopper, however, is the Giant Ocean Tank, where visitors can observe all the animals along a winding walkway leading to the top of the tank. At feeding times, staff dive in, scattering squid for the bigger fish, hand-feeding the sharks and giving the turtles their vitamin-enriched gelatin.

From big screen to deep waters If you want to experience places that cannot be recreated in the aquarium, watch one of the aquatic films showing at the IMAX theater.

HIGHLIGHTS

● Giant Ocean Tank
● Medical Center
● The huge green sea turtle
● Little blue penguins
● Whale-watching trip
● IMAX 3D films

TIPS

● Book two weeks in advance for a special "behind the scenes" tour ($20 per person).
● Check the daily schedule for training sessions, feeding times and shows.

More to See

ADAMS GALLERY

suffolk.edu/adamsgallery

The history and culture of Boston and New England provides plenty of themes for collections and exhibits in this storefront gallery opposite Park Street Church (▷ 56).

➕ J5 ✉ Suffolk University Law School, 120 Tremont Street ☎ 617/305-1782 🕐 Daily 9–7 🚇 Park Street

ARLINGTON STREET CHURCH

ascboston.org

If the church is closed, ask the staff in the office (at the back) to open up. It has what is thought to be the largest collection of Tiffany windows in any one church. A free audio guide describing the windows, can be found on the church's website.

➕ H6 ✉ Boylston Street at Arlington Street. Office: 351 Boylston Street 🕐 Office: Mon–Fri 9–5 🚇 Arlington

BOSTON ATHENAEUM

bostonathenaeum.org

This was the intellectual and cultural heart of the city when it opened in 1807. Members used the library, admired the art collection, met friends and argued beneath the lavishly decorated interiors. Today, anyone can visit the first floor and exhibition galleries, but to appreciate the rare books and works of art, take a free, hour-long Art and Architecture Tour (Tuesday at 5.30, Thursday at 3).

➕ J5 ✉ 101/2 Beacon Street ☎ 617/227-0270, ext. 279 🕐 Tues 12–8, Wed–Sat 10–4 🚇 Park

BOSTON CHILDREN'S MUSEUM

bostonchildrensmuseum.org

Opened in 1913, this is heaven on earth for under-10s. Try the balance climb, play at shops with life-size products, squirt water jets at model boats, stretch a gigantic bubble or just enjoy the play space. When you're all exhausted, retreat to the peaceful Japanese house.

➕ L6 ✉ 308 Congress Street, Museum Wharf ☎ 617/426-6500 🕐 Daily 10–5 (Fri until 9) 🍴 Several nearby 🚇 South Station 💵 Moderate (Fri 5–9 $1)

Colorful neon lights inside the Children's Museum

BOSTON FIRE MUSEUM

bostonfiremuseum.com

Housed in the old firehouse on Congress Street, the museum displays shiny antique fire engines dating back to 1793, a variety of fire alarms and fire-fighting memorabilia from Boston's fires, including the great fire of 1872 and the 1942 Cocoanut Grove disaster.
✚ L6 ✉ 344 Congress Street ☎ 617/338-9700 🕐 Sat 11–4 🚇 South Station
💵 Donation

CHINATOWN

chinatownmainstreet.org

Since the 19th century, Boston's Chinese community has been centered around the blocks between Essex Street and Kneeland Street. Visitors and locals flock to the area, keeping its grocery stores, markets and restaurants humming.
✚ I6 🚇 Chinatown, South Station

IRISH FAMINE MEMORIAL

These bronzes, erected in 1998, commemorate those forced by the 1840s Potato Famine to leave their native Ireland for the United States.
✚ K5 ✉ Washington/School streets

GRANARY BURYING GROUND

If you see only one burial ground, make it this one. Dating from 1660, it's the leafy resting place of many of Boston's big names—Samuel Adams, Paul Revere, James Otis, John Hancock and Peter Faneuil. Throughout, informative sign boards add historic information about the carved headstones, the people buried here and events that shaped early Boston. Many of these help to bring the place and the Colonial era to life.
✚ J5 ✉ 88 Tremont Street 🚇 Park Street

KING'S CHAPEL AND BURYING GROUND

kings-chapel.org

This was built as an Anglican church in 1687 on the orders of King James II, to the indignation of the Puritan colonists. In the town's earliest (1630) burial ground lie two

King's Chapel later became the city's first Unitarian Church

Mayflower passengers and John Winthrop, first governor of Massachusetts.

🚩 K5 ✉ Tremont/School streets ☎ 617/227-2155 🕐 Hours vary–call ahead. No tourists during services 🚇 Park Street

OLD SOUTH MEETING HOUSE

oldsouthmeetinghouse.org

Starting life in 1729 as a Puritan meeting house, this was the site of the meeting that started the historical and pivotal Boston Tea Party in 1773.

🚩 K5 ✉ 310 Washington Street ☎ 617/482-6439 🕐 Apr–Oct daily 9.30–5; Nov–Mar daily 10–4 🚇 State, Downtown Crossing 🎫 Moderate

PARK STREET CHURCH

parkstreet.org

Notable as much for its tall, white steeple as for William Lloyd Garrison's first anti-slavery speech made here in 1829. "My Country 'tis of Thee" was first sung in public here in 1831. An excellent stop for architecture lovers.

🚩 J5 ✉ 1 Park Street 🕐 Jul–Aug Tue–Sat 8–3 🚇 Park Street 🎫 Free

POST OFFICE SQUARE

A charming oasis, with a small café, surrounded by the Downtown area's skyscrapers. It's often filled with office workers at lunchtime, so arrive in late morning or late afternoon to get a park bench and best appreciate the sights and sounds.

🚩 K5 ✉ Between Milk and Franklin streets 🚇 State

ROBERT GOULD SHAW MEMORIAL

A sensitive bronze battle frieze, by the scuptor Augustus Saint-Gaudens, unveiled in 1897 in honor of the Massachusetts 54th Regiment. Shaw, depicted in the film *Glory,* led the Union's first black regiment in the Civil War. Here, for the first time, African Americans were portrayed by a white artist as individuals.

🚩 J5 ✉ Beacon Street, facing State House 🚇 Park Street 🎫 Free

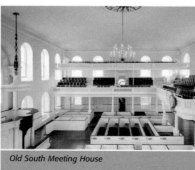

Old South Meeting House

Pausing for a rest at the base of the Robert Gould Shaw Monument

Walk This Way

The areas around Boston Common and the Waterfront are some of the most pedestrian-friendly, with historic stops and shopping.

DISTANCE: 0.8 miles (1.3km) **ALLOW:** 2–4 hours

START

BOSTON COMMON
(▷ 50) 🚇 J6 🚇 Boylston

END

NEW ENGLAND AQUARIUM
(▷ 53) 🚇 L5 🚇 Aquarium

❶ From the Boylston T stop, walk left for about a block on Tremont Street, cross Tremont, and take your first right on Avery Street. You will pass the Ritz-Carlton on your right.

❽ Across from City Hall, cross Congress Street to Faneuil Hall (▷ 26). On the other side of Faneuil Hall, cross the street to the New England Aquarium (▷ 53).

❷ Where Avery street ends, take a right onto Washington Street, followed by a left onto Essex Street. Follow Essex Street into Chinatown, where you could stop for a meal.

❼ Follow Washington to State Street and take a right. Where State meets Congress Street, take a left. City Hall will be on your left.

❸ Two blocks down Essex Street, take a left onto Chauncy Street. Follow it to Summer Street, and take a left.

❻ Follow Washington to the right. Pass the Diamond District at 333 Washington—full of jewelry bargains (▷ panel, 58).

❹ After one block you will hit Downtown Crossing. This is the center of bargain shopping in Boston.

❺ Continue up Washington several blocks to the Old South Meeting House (▷ 56).

Shopping

BOSTON CHILDREN'S MUSEUM SHOP

theshopatbcm.ordercompletion.com

From books to games to educational toys, the museum is the ideal place to pick up something special for youngsters.

➕ L6 ✉ 308 Congress Street ☎ 617/426-6500 🚇 South Station

BRATTLE BOOK SHOP

brattlebookshop.com

A treasure trove of rare and secondhand books with a good section on Boston and New England. It's been in business since the 19th century, so count on finding plenty of out-of-print and rare books, plus academic works, maps and old leather-bound books.

➕ J5 ✉ 9 West Street ☎ 617/542-0210 🚇 Park Street

BROMFIELD PEN SHOP

bromfieldpenshop.com

This quaint shop sells everything from from vintage early 1900s models to new Montblanc and Cross and cheap disposables, as well as desk accessories, watches and other gift items.

➕ J5 ✉ 5 Bromfield Street ☎ 617/482-9053 🚇 Park Street

DOWNTOWN CROSSING

downtowncrossing.org

This shopping area, encompassing parts of Washington, Winter and Bromfield streets, is home to street fashion, shoes, jewelry, cameras and the like, plus the city's main department stores.

➕ J6 🚇 Downtown Crossing

FOOT PATHS

footpathsshoes.com

A great place to pick up elegant, casual and athletic shoes for both men and women, all the big names are here plus a full range of hiking boots.

➕ K6 ✉ 415 Washington Street ☎ 617/338-6008 🚇 Downtown Crossing

ICA STORE

icastore.org

Arguably the most exciting design gift shop in Boston, the ICA Store carries a stunning selection of jewelry, household decor items, children's toys, accessories and books on art and design.

➕ L6 ✉ 100 Northern Avenue ☎ 617/478-3104 🚇 Courthouse

ST. JOHN BOUTIQUE

stjohnknits.com

St. John was founded in 1962 by Robert and Marie Gray and now has stores all over the globe. It is filled with elegant, couture knitwear for women.

➕ H6 ✉ 292 Boylston Street ☎ 617/338-6130 🚇 Arlington

THE TANNERY

thetannery.com

With a staff dedicated to finding the perfect fit for each and every customer's foot, this is the place to pick up both rugged outdoor shoes and casual numbers alike.

➕ H6 ✉ 711 Boylston Street ☎ 617/267-5500 🚇 Arlington

DOWNTOWN BARGAINS

Downtown Crossing, and all around Washington Street, is known as prime bargain territory for the marked-down jewelry sold at the **Diamond District** (at 333 Washington Street). Other discounts nearby: designer men's and women's shoes at DSW Shoe (385 Washington Street) and outdoor gear at Eddie Bauer Outlet (500 Washington Street).

Entertainment and Nightlife

BOSTON OPERA HOUSE

bostonoperahouse.com

Originally a vaudeville theater, this grand showroom now features Broadway touring productions, as well as the Boston Ballet's annual Christmas performances of *The Nutcracker*.

🔲 K6 ✉ 539 Washington Street ☎ 617/259-3400 🅿 Chinatown, Boylston

CHARLES PLAYHOUSE

blueman.com

Shear Madness, a comedy whodunnit set in a hairdresser's, has played here since 1980. *Blue Man Group*, another long-running show, presents its offbeat mix of visually stunning theater, music and performance art on the Charles's other stage.

🔲 J6 ✉ 74 Warrenton Street ☎ 617/426-5225 *(Shear Madness)*; 617/426-6912 *(Blue Man Group)* 🅿 Boylston

CUTLER MAJESTIC THEATRE

cutlermajestic.org

Visiting dance troupes, world music performers, Shakespearean actors and Emerson College student productions all use the stage at this 1903 venue.

🔲 J6 ✉ 219 Tremont Street ☎ 617/824-8000 🅿 Boylston

DICK DOHERTY'S COMEDY DEN

dickdoherty.com

A leading full-service comedy venue, beneath a lively club that features established and upcoming comics.

🔲 J6 ✉ 184 High Street ☎ 800/401-2221 🕐 Shows daily 🅿 Aquarium

EMERSON COLONIAL THEATRE

emersoncolonialtheatre.com

This lush, beautifully restored, turn-of-the-20th-century theater stages pre-Broadway productions (so you can enjoy the hits first!) as well as a range of other performing arts events.

🔲 J6 ✉ 106 Boylston Street ☎ 877/613-0134 🅿 Boylston

HUB PUB

thehubpub.com

Close to the Theater District, this is a busy pub popular with sports fans making use of the TVs. Hearty food is served until 1am every night of the week.

🔲 K5 ✉ 18 Province Street ☎ 617/227-8952 🅿 Park

JACQUE'S CABARET

jacques-cabaret.com

Female impersonators and other offbeat performances draw everyone from drag queens to bachelorette parties.

🔲 J6 ✉ 79 Broadway ☎ 617/426-8902 🅿 Arlington

JM CURLEY

jmcurleyboston.com

Named for James Michael Curley, the controversial but popular mayor of Boston, who was once re-elected while in jail, this pub has a great vibe and great pub food.

🔲 J5 ✉ 21 Temple Place ☎ 617/338-5333 🅿 Park

TICKETS

BosTix sell half-price theater tickets on the day of the show (from 11am). As a fully fledged Ticketmaster outlet, it also sells full-price tickets in advance for venues in Boston and the rest of New England. Booths are at: ✉ Faneuil Hall Marketplace 🕐 Tue–Sun 10–4 ✉ Copley Square 🕐 Thu– Fri, 11–5; Sat–Sun 10–4. Tickets cover theater, concerts, museums, sports events and trolley tours. Cash and credit cards are accepted.

NICK'S COMEDY STOP

nickscomedystop.com

For over 35 years this well-loved Theater District comedy club has hosted local and would-be comedy stars on stage.
J6 ✉ 100 Warrenton Street ☎ 617/830-2551 Ⓐ Boylston

ROWES WHARF BAR AT BOSTON HARBOR HOTEL

bhh.com

Sophisticated and comfortable, Rowes Wharf Bar serves classic Boston pub fare, fine blended and single-malt scotch and serious martinis.
L5 ✉ 70 Rowes Wharf ☎ 617/439-7000 Ⓐ Aquarium

ROYALE BOSTON

royaleboston.com

With its edgy live bands and cutting-edge DJs, the crowded and loud Royale is Boston's No.1 megaclub.
J6 ✉ 279 Tremont Street ☎ 617/338-7699 Ⓐ Boylston, Chinatown

SCHOLARS AMERICAN BISTRO & COCKTAIL LOUNGE

scholarsbostonbistro.com

From electro house to jazz brunches, this central pub/cocktail bar and pool hall is always humming, especially after work. It also serves good-value food.
K5 ✉ 25 School Street ☎ 617/248-0025 Ⓐ Park

SILVERTONE BAR & GRILL

silverstonedowntown.com

Popular subterranean joint just off the Common features comfy booths, creative martinis and a bar menu of comfort food. It often gets crowded on weekends.
K5 ✉ 69 Bromfield Street ☎ 617/338-7887 Ⓐ Park Street

W LOUNGE

starwoodhotels.com

With its oversized sofas and cheerful fire pit and romantic ambience, all that is needed is the signature W cocktail.
J6 ✉ W Hotel, 100 Stuart Street ☎ 617/310-6790 Ⓐ Chinatown

THE WANG THEATRE

bochcenter.org

A gloriously renovated 1920s 3,500-seat movie palace used for concerts, opera, Broadway shows and dance.
J6 ✉ 270 Tremont Street ☎ 617/482-9393 Ⓐ Boylston

WHISKY SAIGON

whiskysaigon.com

This fashionable spot features some of Boston's best DJs, with state-of-the-art surround-sound and special effects.
J6 ✉ 116 Boylston Street ☎ 617/482-7799 Ⓐ Boylston

THE WILBUR

thewilbur.com

The century-old Wilbur theater regularly hosts some of America's finest comedians as well as music acts such as The Temptations and Judy Collins.
J6 ✉ 246 Tremont Street ☎ 617/248-9700 Ⓐ Boylston

CHEAP THEATER

Productions in the Theater District can be expensive, but many college theater groups offer fine productions at lower prices. For example, the **Playwrights' Theatre** at Boston University (949 Commonwealth Avenue, 617/358-7529) showcases plays written or produced by students or alumni. Particularly popular is the annual **Boston Theater Marathon,** which features 50 10-minute plays every spring.

Where to Eat

<table>
<tr><td colspan="2">PRICES</td></tr>
<tr><td colspan="2">Prices are approximate, based on a 3-course meal for one person.</td></tr>
<tr><td>$$$</td><td>over $40</td></tr>
<tr><td>$$</td><td>$20–$40</td></tr>
<tr><td>$</td><td>under $20</td></tr>
</table>

BARKING CRAB ($)

barkingcrab.com

A rough-and-ready clam shack where you can eat indoors or alfresco, with downtown views across the water. Go expecting crowds, a wait and noise but mostly lots of fun.

➕ I6 ✉ 88 Sleeper Street, off Northern Avenue, Waterfront ☎ 617/426-2722 🕐 From 11.30am 🚇 South Station

BISTRO DU MIDI ($$)

bistrodumidi.com

French Provincial cuisine is served in an exceptional location overlooking the Public Garden with a street-level bar offering food and drink. There is also an upstairs Garden-view French-styled dining room with wooden beams and fireplace, as well as a pretty outdoor patio.

➕ H6 ✉ 272 Boylston Street, Theater District ☎ 617/426-7878 🕐 Lunch, dinner daily 🚇 Arlington

THE BRISTOL LOUNGE ($$$)

fourseasons.com/boston/dining

Overlooking the Public Garden and known as much for the service as the food, this is one of Boston's best formal restaurants. Upscale comfort food, including the Bristol Burger, homemade pasta and fresh seafood are as good as the excellent cocktails.

➕ J6 ✉ Four Seasons Hotel, 200 Boylston Street ☎ 617/351-2037 🕐 Breakfast, lunch, dinner daily, Sun brunch 🚇 Arlington

CAFÉ FLEURI ($$)

langhamhotels.com

Bright and open, this smart atrium café specializes in dishes created to showcase seasonal local ingredients. The Saturday Chocolate Bar is a decadent buffet of chocolate desserts, while Sunday brunch is one of the city's best.

➕ K5 ✉ The Langham Boston, 250 Franklin Street ☎ 617/956-8751 🕐 Breakfast and lunch daily 🚇 Downtown Crossing

DORETTA TAVERNA & RAW BAR ($$)

dorettaboston.com

Chef and restaurateur Michael Schlow transformed his former Italian restaurant here into a Greek one, with a contemporary Mediterranean menu featuring tasty classics such as feta-stuffed figs and grilled octopus with capers and onion.

➕ H6 ✉ 79 Park Plaza ☎ 617/422-0008 🕐 Lunch Mon–Fri, dinner Mon–Sat. Closed Sun 🚇 Arlington

DUMPLING CAFE ($)

dumplingcafe.com

This Taiwanese/Chinese restaurant specializes in delicious Mini Juicy Buns (soup dumplings) made with noodle wrappers filled with pork and a tasty broth. Staying open until 2am, this is a great late-night spot.

➕ I6 ✉ 695 Washington Street ☎ 617//338-8859 🕐 Lunch, dinner daily 🚇 Chinatown

ESPRESSO LOVE ($)

espressolove.com

The city version of a Martha's Vineyard favorite, serving great coffee and freshly baked muffins and breads.

➕ K5 ✉ 33 Broad Street ☎ 857/284-7462 🕐 Mon–Fri 6.30–6 🚇 State/Aquarium

GRILL 23 & BAR ($$$)

grill23.com

This excellent locally owned steak house specializes in organic, sustainable and humanely raised meats, as well as local seafood and seasonal ingredients. The service is as outstanding, as the wine list.

➕ H6 ✉ 161 Berkeley Street (at Stuart Street) ☎ 617/542-2255 🕐 Dinner daily 🚇 Arlington

LEGAL HARBORSIDE ($$)

legalseafoods.com

This enormous three-floor facility is the flagship of the Legal Sea Foods restaurant dynasty. Level 3 is a rooftop bar and lounge, with awesome views of the waterfront through the three walls of windows and the two patios. Level 1 has a fish market, tables overlooking the marina and its signature seafood menu.

➕ L6 ✉ 270 Northern Avenue ☎ 617470-2900 🕐 Lunch, dinner daily (till late) 🚇 South Station

MARLIAVE ($$–$$$)

marliave.com

The osso buco and risotto, onion soup and escargots reflect the menu's French and Italian inspiration, but there are familiar American favorites, with pastrami and Reuben sandwiches. All the breads are made inhouse, along with desserts, sauces, pasta and ice cream. At the raw bar, check out the $1 "happy hour" for local oysters and clams.

➕ J5 ✉ 10 Bosworth Street ☎ 617/422-0004 🕐 Daily 11–10 🚇 Park

NEW JUMBO SEAFOOD ($)

newjumboseafoodboston.com

Crowds flock to this enclave of superlative Chinese food for the superfresh, water-tank-straight-to-wok shrimp, lobster and flounder dishes. Be sure to try the delicious giant clams in blackbean sauce.

➕ J6 ✉ 5 Hudson Street ☎ 617/542-2823 🕐 Lunch, dinner daily 🚇 Chinatown

NEW SHANGHAI ($)

bostonnewshanghai.com

This is an upscale Chinatown eatery, specializing in Shanghai-style cuisine with good service. Cold appetizers include eggplant with garlic sauce.

➕ J6 ✉ 21 Hudson Street ☎ 617/338-6688 🕐 Lunch, dinner daily 🚇 Chinatown

ROW 34 ($$$)

row34.com

Seafood lovers should head straight to Row 34 for some of the freshest, most delicious seafood in town. The menu boasts a great raw bar selection, as well as craft beers.

➕ L6 ✉ 383 Congress Street ☎ 617/553-5900 🕐 Lunch and dinner daily, brunch Sun 🚇 South Station

ROWES WHARF SEA GRILLE ($$)

roweswharfseagrille.com

Boston Harbor Hotel's waterside barrestaurant and patio is one of the town's finest casual options—for both its topnotch shrimp cocktail and its breezy, flower-festooned outdoor patio.

➕ L5 ✉ 70 Rowes Wharf ☎ 617/856-7744 🕐 Breakfast, lunch, afternoon tea, dinner daily 🚇 Aquarium

TEATRO ($$–$$$)

teatroboston.com

A beautiful, blue-lit boîte filled with theater-going crowds who are here for the authentic Italian menu. The freshly made pasta dishes are delicious.

➕ J6 ✉ 177 Tremont Street, Downtown ☎ 617/778-6841 🕐 Dinner Tue–Sun 🚇 Park Street

Home to some of the finest shopping and people-watching in all the city, Back Bay and the South End are also vibrant residential neighborhoods.

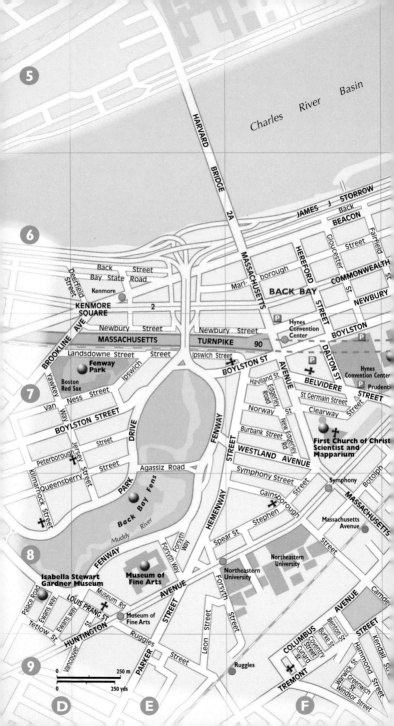

5

Charles River Basin

HARVARD BRIDGE
2A

JAMES J STORROW

Back
BEACON

Fairfield

Street

6

Back Street

Bay State Road

Deerfield Street

Kenmore

KENMORE SQUARE

2

Newbury Street

MASSACHUSETTS

Marl-borough

Gloucester

Street

HEREFORD

STREET

BACK BAY

COMMONWEALTH

NEWBURY

St

Hynes
Convention
Center

Newbury Street

TURNPIKE 90

BOYLSTON

DALTON ST

Ipswich Street

BROOKLINE AVE

Landsdowne Street

Street

Fenway Park

Boston
Red Sox

Yawkey
Way

Van Ness Street

BOYLSTON STREET

Jersey Street

Ipswich

Street

BOYLSTON ST

Haviland St

Edgerley
Road

Norway

Burbank Street

St Germain Street

New Edgerley St

AVENUE

BELVIDERE

Clearway

STREET

Hynes
Convention
Center

Prudenti

**First Church of Christ
Scientist and
Mapparium**

7

Peterborough Street

Queensberry Street

Street

Kilmarnock Street

DRIVE

PARK

Agassiz Road

Back Bay Fens

Muddy River

FENWAY

FENWAY STREET

WESTLAND AVENUE

Symphony Street

HEMENWAY STREET

Spear St

Norway St

Gainsborough Street

Stephen

Symphony

Massachusetts
Avenue

MASSACHUSETTS

Botolph

8

**Isabella Stewart
Gardner Museum**

Palace Road

Evans Way

Tetlow St.

LOUIS PRANG ST

HUNTINGTON

Museum Rd

**Museum of
Fine Arts**

Forsyth Way

Forsyth Street

AVENUE

**Museum of
Fine Arts**

Vancouver

Ruggles

Street

Northeastern
University

Northeastern
University

Leon Street

Forsyth Street

Benton St

Burke St

Coventry Street

Cunard Street

AVENUE

Camde

Hammond St

9

0   250 m
0   250 yds

PARKER

Street

Ruggles

COLUMBUS

TREMONT

Warwick St

Greenwich
St

Windsor Street

Kendall Stu

STREET

D   **E**   **F**

Map labels

Charles River Esplanade

EMBANKMENT ROAD

Charles River Embankment

Storrow Lagoon

Gibson House

MEMORIAL DRIVE 1

Street

STREET

BERKELEY

EXETER

DARTMOUTH

Marlborough Street

STREET

Commonwealth Avenue

CLARENDON STREET

Copley Theater

BERKELEY STREET

AVENUE

Newbury Street

STREET

Trinity Church and Copley Square

Providence Street

AVENUE

Copley

ST

JAMES

Lyric Stage

STREET

Hancock Tower

Stuart Street

28

Boston Public Library

Back Bay Station

STREET

CLARENDON AVENUE

Prudential Center and Skywalk

DARTMOUTH

AVENUE

Copley Place

BACK BAY STATION

COLUMBUS

STREET

CHANDLER STREET

Harcourt St

Carlton St

HUNTINGTON

Yarmouth Street

West

STREET

Appleton Street

Lawrence St

Street

Gray Street

Gray Street

Boston Center for the Arts

Braddock Parkway

Holyoke Street

AVENUE

Warren

Dwight Street

Milford Street

Durham Street

NEWTON

Canton

Warren Avenue

Montgomery St

TREMONT

Hanson Street

Waltham Street

Bradford St

W. Rutland Square

GREENWICH Square

Pembroke Street

West Brookline

Union Street

AVENUE

Union Pk

STREET

CONCORD SQUARE

Street

DEDHAM STREET

Street

COLUMBUS PKWY

Claremont Pk

Rutland Square

Street

SHAWMUT

WASHINGTON STREET

Park

AVENUE

Street

MONSIGNOR REYNOLDS WAY

MALDEN ST

TREMONT

WEST CONCORD STREET

Rutland Street

Blackstone Square

SOUTH END

HARRISON

Plympton Street

Wareham Street

AVENUE

Springfield

Franklin Square

East Brookline Street

E Dedham Street

Northampton

AVENUE

EAST NEWTON

St George St

E Canton Street

Street

SHAWMUT

WASHINGTON

Worcester Square

EAST CONCORD STREET

STREET

ALBANY

Lenox Street

Ramsey Park

G   H

Boston Public Library

From left: The illuminated marble staircase and cloisters

THE BASICS

bpl.org

➕ G6

✉ Copley Square

☎ 617/536-5400

🕐 Mon–Thu 9–9, Fri–Sat 9–5, Sun 1–5

🍴 On premises

Ⓒ Copley

♿ Good

💲 Free

❓ Tours (Dartmouth Street entrance) Mon 2.30, Tue, Thu 6, Fri–Sat 11; also Sun 2. Lectures

HIGHLIGHTS

- Puvis de Chavannes murals
- John Singer Sargent murals
- Daniel Chester French bronze doors
- The courtyard

TIP

- Free lunchtime concerts in the courtyard on Fridays in the summer.

This is no ordinary library. Behind its granite facade lies an opulent institution built in Renaissance palazzo style and decorated with sculptures and paintings by some of the best artists of the day.

The education of the people A people's palace dedicated to the advancement of learning was what Charles Follen McKim was commissioned to design. Facing H.H. Richardson's Trinity Church across Copley Square, it opened its doors to the public in 1895. It is now the Research Library, the General Library being housed in the adjoining Johnson Building.

Further treasures Pass between Bela Pratt's voluptuous bronzes, *Science* and *Art* (1912), to enter through Daniel Chester French's bronze doors. Ascend the marble staircase, guarded by lions, and from its windows catch a glimpse of the peaceful courtyard. The stairs and landing are decorated with panels by Puvis de Chavannes, whimsical representations of the muses of inspiration. The Abbey Room has paintings depicting the quest for the Holy Grail, by Edwin Austin Abbey. Bates Hall is a magnificent room; get a close-up view of its barrel-vaulted ceiling from the stairs that lead up to the Sargent Gallery. The John Singer Sargent murals, *Triumph of Religion,* were completed in 1919. Pause to sit in the colonnaded courtyard, watching the fountain and enjoying the tranquility.

Commonwealth Avenue

A Parisian-style boulevard lined with the grandest houses in Boston is at the heart of an amazing piece of 19th-century urban planning. To walk down it is to be transported to a different age.

Landfill By the1850s, Boston was getting over-crowded. Desperate for land, developers turned to the swampy "back bay" of the Charles River, embarking on a remarkable landfill project to create a new residential district. Inspired by Paris's boulevard system, the architect Arthur Gilman planned a grid, eight blocks long and four blocks wide, with a long central mall.

Commonwealth Avenue The wealthy industrialists who flocked to the Back Bay felt some of the Puritan restraints of the Proper Bostonians of Beacon Hill, and their rows of ostentatious brownstones are a somewhat sub-dued blend of Victorian styles. The centerpiece is Commonwealth Avenue. Central gardens are lined with trees; in spring magnolias bloom in profusion. The Boston Women's Memorial lies between Fairfield and Gloucester streets. Most houses are now apartments but the château-like Burrage Mansion at Hereford Street stands out, with statuettes everywhere. Visit Gibson House (▷ 78) to see a more average home.

Feeling fit? The mall is just part of a 7-mile (11km) long Emerald Necklace of green space stretching from Boston Common to Franklin Park.

THE BASICS

✚ G6

🚊 Newbury and Boylston streets

🚇 Arlington, Copley, Hynes Convention Center

HIGHLIGHTS

● Magnolias in spring on Commonwealth Avenue
● Lights on the mall at Christmas
● Memorial to firemen killed in the Hotel Vendome fire

TIPS

● More intimate than Commonwealth Avenue and no less beautiful is next-door Marlborough Street, which is lined with flowering dogwoods in the springtime.
● North–south streets are named alphabetically, Arlington to Hereford.

Fenway Park

Fenway Park is home to the city's beloved Red Sox

THE BASICS

boston.redsox.mlb.com/
bos/ballpark/information

🚻 E7

✉ 4 Yawkey Way

☎ 877/733-7699

🕐 Hours vary, depending on game and event

🍴 Variety of options. $-$$

🚇 Kenmore Square Station

♿ Excellent

💰 Expensive

❓ Regular 60-min tours 9–5 (or four hours before game time). Call to confirm tours are running (events and weather can impact tours)

HIGHLIGHT

● The lone red seat in the right-field bleachers is where Ted Williams's famous 502-foot homerun hit landed on June 9, 1946

TIP

● Grab a last-minute game ticket at Gate E two hours before the game.

In a city where sports are revered, Fenway Park is the pinnacle of the city's sports arenas. Even those who don't follow baseball can appreciate the historic park where the Boston Red Sox have played since 1912.

Take me out to the ball game Fenway Park is a mecca for baseball fans, who love to catch a Red Sox game at the oldest Major League Baseball ballpark in the country. There are lots of quirky things about the park, which was added to the National Register of Historic Places in 2012.

Meet a monster Its major feature, the 37-foot-high (11m) "Green Monster," wall towers over left field. Seats atop the wall are quite popular. The Green Monster is just 310 feet (94m) away from home plate (the standard is 25), so right-handed hitters love to aim for it to get a home run. Not everyone knows that the wall was only painted green in 1947.

The curse More than anything else over the years, though, Fenway Park is known for its long 86-year losing streak, which was broken in 2004. Blamed on the "Curse of the Bambino," which supposedly happened when the Red Sox traded Babe Ruth away to the New York Yankees (Boston's biggest rival), the curse was reversed in a game against the St. Louis Cardinals in the World Series. The Red Sox won again in 2007 and in 2013.

From left: El Jaleo by John Singer Sargent; the interior facade that overlooks the courtyard

Isabella Stewart Gardner Museum

The woman who created this collection had a passion for art and horticulture. Her finds are arranged in a Venetian-style *palazzo* built around a courtyard.

Beautiful things Determined to give her country world-class art, Mrs Gardner made a start in 1896 by buying a Rembrandt self-portrait. Her collection grew to include work by Vermeer, Giotto, Botticelli, Raphael, Degas and Matisse, as well as John Singer Sargent and James McNeill Whistler. She also bought prints and drawings, books, sculptures, ceramics and glass, tapestries, stained glass and furniture.

Music and horticulture The building itself, known as Fenway Court, and the atmosphere that pervades it, is as much the creation of Mrs Gardner as her collection. She arranged her objects in a series of rooms—the Raphael Room, the Gothic Room, the intimate Blue Room and more. She filled the courtyard with sculptures, plants and trees, and she celebrated the opening of her home (she lived on the top floor) to the public with a concert given by members of the Boston Symphony Orchestra. Today, concerts are held in the Calderwood Hall on Sundays from September to May.

Art heist Still America's biggest art theft, in March 1990 thieves dressed as policemen stole 13 items, which have not been recovered. Among them were a priceless Vermeer and *The Sea of Galilee,* Rembrandt's only seascape.

THE BASICS

gardnermuseum.org

⊞ D8

✉ 280 The Fenway

☎ 617/566-1401

🕐 Wed–Mon 11–5 (Thu till 9). Closed Tue except most public hols

🍴 On premises

Ⓜ Museum of Fine Arts

⅃ Good

💲 Expensive

❓ Concerts: Sep–May Sun 1.30 (☎ 617/278 5156). Courtyard: talks most weekdays (times posted at the information desk). Audio tours $4. Lectures, shop

HIGHLIGHT

● Renzo Piano's wing provides a restaurant, greenhouses and more

TIP

● In some of the rooms you must pull back curtains and open drawers to see the objects that are protected from the light.

Museum of Fine Arts

The Museum of Fine Arts is one of America's foremost museums. The Asian collection is unrivaled in this hemisphere, the European art is superb and the American rooms are excellent.

Asian, Egyptian, Classical The MFA's Nubian collection is the best outside the Sudan. It is all exquisite, from the neat rows of little *shawabtis* (figurines) to the jewelry. The Egyptian rooms are popular, with mummies, hieroglyphics and splendid Old Kingdom sculptures. Buddhist sculptures, Chinese ceramics and Indian paintings form part of an Asian collection.

European In the European galleries, seek out the little gem of a Rembrandt in a glass case, then take in works of Tiepolo, Gainsborough,

Turner, Delacroix, Constable and a good number of Millets. The Impressionist room is an array of familiar paintings, with works from Monet, Renoir and Gauguin. There is porcelain from all over Europe.

American The spectacular Art of the Americas wing showcases more than 16,000 works of art from South, Central and North America. The collection includes art in all media displayed chronologically in 49 galleries, beginning with ancient Mayan ceramics through the late 20th-century art of Jackson Pollack. There are also major pieces of silver by Paul Revere, portraits by John Singleton Copley and John Singer Sargent and landscapes by Georgia O'Keeffe. Furniture and decorative arts are featured in nine period rooms.

THE BASICS

mfa.org

✚ E8

✉ 465 Huntington Avenue

☎ 617/267-9300

🕐 Mon–Tue 10–4.45, Wed–Fri 10–9.45, Sat–Sun 10–4.45

🍴 Choice on premises

🚇 Museum of Fine Arts

♿ Excellent

💲 Expensive. Wed 4–9.45 voluntary contribution. Boston CityPass applies

❓ Regular free guided tours Mon–Sat. Film programs Thu–Sun. Lectures, concerts. Good shop

Newbury Street

Newbury Street houses retail and residential buildings

THE BASICS

newbury-st.com

🔳 G6

✉ Between Arlington Street and Massachusetts Avenue

🕙 Most shops open 10–6

🍴 Excellent bistros line each side of the street

🚇 Arlington, Copley, Massachusetts Avenue

♿ Fair to excellent, depending on the business. Many have elevators

HIGHLIGHTS

● Window-shopping in Newbury Street
● People-watching in the Newbury Street cafés
● At 39 Newbury Street, Shreve, Crump & Low is known for its Gurgling Cod pitchers, modeled after English "glug jugs"

Bustling Newbury Street in the Back Bay is the place to go to shop, eat, drink and while away the afternoon at a cozy sidewalk café. Its eight blocks are packed with everything from high-end boutiques, selling a vast range of clothes and jewelry, to art galleries, featuring fine paintings and sculptures.

Galleries Many a pleasant hour can be spent browsing in the galleries and stopping off in a café now and then. Individual small shops are housed in beautiful historic houses. A concentration of galleries lies between Arlington and Fairfield streets. They display works by 19th- and 20th-century artists, in addition to contemporary pieces. The Robert Klein Gallery, at 38 Newbury Street, is the only major art gallery in New England dedicated to fine art photography. If you are interested in avant-garde galleries explore the South End, particularly around Harrison and Thayer streets.

Shop, shop, shop Shopping is also an enormous draw of the area. At the intersection with Arlington Street, where shops tend to be high-end and high-priced, you'll find plenty of international jewelry shops, fashion designers and day spas. These give way to more mid-range shops as you move toward the other end of the street, which intersects with Massachusetts Avenue. On the way there, cross mainstream fashion chains, gift shops and boutiques.

From left: The view
from the tower at
night; retail outlets; the
Prudential Tower

TOP
25

Prudential Center
and Skywalk

This building gives you stunning views of Boston and the New England countryside from its 50th floor. Drop back closer to the ground for shops and eating places.

Skywalk at the Prudential The Prudential Tower is part of the 1960s Prudential Center office and shopping complex. Take the elevator to the Skywalk on the 50th floor and you have stunning 360-degree views, weather permitting, as far as the mountains of New Hampshire. Pick out the gold dome of the State House; peer down on the rooftops of the neat Back Bay homes and over the Charles River to MIT and Cambridge; see the parks of the Emerald Necklace stretching into the distance; look out to the Boston Harbor Islands. Interactive exhibits cover key historical and sporting events, as well as distinguished buildings and residents. Looking to relax while soaking up that same stunning view? The Top of the Hub restaurant, on the Pru's 52nd floor, looks out to the twinkling city and beyond; be sure to stop in for a cocktail or dessert, and a city profile you won't soon forget.

Down to earth Meanwhile, on the lower levels of the building, find plenty of indoor shopping and snacking. There are several dining options, including Eataly (▷ 84), an enormous Italian marketplace with both to-go and sit-down restaurants. Stores lure shoppers in for high-end jewelry, international fashions, quality stationery and flowers.

THE BASICS

skywalkboston.com
➕ G7
✉ Prudential Tower, 800 Boylston Street
☎ 617/859-0648
🕐 Daily 10–10. Skywalk: Mar–Oct 10–9.30, Nov–Feb 10–8
🍴 Top of the Hub; choice in Prudential Center
🚇 Prudential, Hynes Convention Center
♿ Excellent
✋ Expensive. Boston CityPass applies

HIGHLIGHTS

● Views from the Pru after snow
● Views from the Pru at night
● Top of the Hub bar and restaurant on the 52nd floor
● Don't miss the two short films included with admission: *Wings Over Boston* and *Dreams of Freedom*
● Live jazz nightly in the Top of the Hub lounge

The South End

● Excellent bistros and restaurants on Tremont and Washington streets
● Cutting-edge art galleries, unique gift shops and home stores

TIPS

● Be sure to make a reservation before visiting the area's restaurants: tables fill up fast.
● Every Sunday, from May-October, SOWA Open Market features local artists, farmers, chefs, brewers and musicians.

First occupied by musicians and teachers in the 1850s, the South End is the preserve of young professionals and artists once again.

Residential It is a lively residential area, whose elegant bow-fronted terraces, many profusely decorated with balustrades and window boxes, line leafy streets and squares. Running through the middle is Tremont Street, where local shops are punctuated by great places to eat. There is a broad ethnic mix here and a strong gay community. The South End has a large number of art galleries, particularly around Harrison and Thayer streets. The neighborhood lies between Huntington Avenue and the Expressway. Its main commercial streets are Washington Street, Tremont Street, and Columbus Avenue.

SoWa The most rapidly changing area of the South End is the SoWa district (so named because it sits South of Washington Street). Blessed with fashionable restaurants and cafés—from The Gallows to Flour Bakery (both ▷ 84)—the area currently has some of the most expensive real estate and most adventurous interior design in the city, but it has still not been entirely gentrified (a fact that locals say lends it an urbane, gritty feel).

By day and by night Walk the neighborhood's parks during the day, admire its rooftops and the tiny gardens in front of its brownstones, visit its trendy art galleries and home-goods shops, then stay to enjoy dinner in its stylish restaurants. Spring and summer bring elaborate gardens into bloom and fine alfresco dining.

THE BASICS

south-end-boston.com

✚ H8

✉ Between the Greenway and Massachusetts Avenue

🕓 Most shops open 10–6. Most restaurants open 5pm–midnight

🍽 Excellent bistros line each side of the street

🚇 Back Bay Station, New England Medical Center

♿ Fair to excellent, depending on the business. Many have elevators

Trinity Church and Copley Square

HIGHLIGHTS

Trinity Church
● Polychrome interior
● John La Farge paintings and lancet windows
● Lantern tower
● Christmas candlelight services

TIPS

● Free guided tours of Trinity Church on Sundays after regular service.
● Guided and self-guided tours are available for a fee other days, call for times.

H.H. Richardson's prototype French Romanesque church is often described as America's masterpiece of ecclesiastical architecture. It faces Copley Square, home to the Boston Public Library.

Trinity Church The Back Bay was a newly developed landfill area when in 1872 Henry Hobson Richardson was commissioned to draw up designs for a new Trinity Church. A massive lantern tower over the transept crossing dominates the church inside and out, requiring more than 2,000 wooden piles massed together to support its granite foundations. Outside, the granite blocks are broken up by bands of pink sandstone. Inside, John La Farge created an intricate polychrome interior, a tapestry of reds and greens highlighted with gold. The church

also contains several important examples of La Farge's groundbreaking stained-glass work. In the baptistery is a bust by Daniel Chester French of the portly rector Phillips Brooks, who composed the popular carol "O Little Town of Bethlehem."

John Hancock Tower There is something very serene about this icy shaft of blue glass, designed by Henry Cobb, of I.M. Pei & Partners. The building caused a big sensation at first. You can't go inside, but you can still admire the tower from the outside, watching the reflections of the other buildings nearby and snapping photos of what it shows. In Copley Square Plaza, look for the Tortoise and the Hare stature, which commemorate the runners in the Boston Marathon. The finish line is steps away.

THE BASICS

Trinity Church
trinitychurchboston.org
✚ G6
✉ Copley Square
☎ 617/536-0944
🕐 Daily 8–6
🚇 Copley
♿ Good
✋ Free
❓ Free half-hour organ recitals Fri 12.15 (dona tions welcome). Sun services 7.45, 9, 11.15 (with choir music), 6

John Hancock Tower
✚ H6
✉ Copley Square
🍴 Nearby
🚇 Copley

More to See

BACK BAY FENS

Once a saltwater bay, this was the first of Frederick Law Olmsted's string of parks, that became known as the Emerald Necklace. Stroll along the banks of Muddy River through the willows or sit in the Rose Garden.

E8 ⊠ The Fenway/Park Drive Hynes Convention Center, Museum of Fine Arts

CHARLES RIVER ESPLANADE

This 3-mile (4.8km) public green space stretches along the edge of Charles River from the Museum of Science to the Boston University Bridge, and is a great for a bike ride or stroll. It is home to the Hatch Memorial Shell, which hosts events.

H5 ⊠ Storrow Memorial Drive Charles/MGH

FIRST CHURCH OF CHRIST, SCIENTIST AND THE MAPPARIUM

tfccs.com; marybakereddylibrary.org

The scale of this complex is mind-blowing. The world headquarters for the Church of Christ, Scientist, occupies 4 acres (1.6ha) of prime Back Bay land, with a church seating 3,000. The Mother Church of Christian Science was founded in Boston in 1892 by Mary Baker Eddy. The 1930s Mapparium, on the first floor of the Mary Baker Eddy Library, is a brightly colored stained-glass globe that's so huge you can actually walk inside it.

F7 ⊠ 175 Huntington Avenue; Library: 200 Massachusetts Avenue ☎ 617/450-2000 Church: daily. Library: Tue–Sun 10–4 Prudential Library: moderate

GIBSON HOUSE

This time capsule of a home perfectly preserves what life in Boston's Victorian era looked like. It was built in 1860 and filled with items like an original 1795 Willard clock, artwork and 19th century family heirlooms.

H5 ⊠ 137 Beacon Street 617/267–6338 Tours Wed–Sun at 1, 2 and 3 and by appointment Moderate Arlington Street Station

The Mapparium, a huge stained-glass globe

South End Stroll

You will see Victorian architecture, boutiques, restaurants and parks. Make sure you leave time to stop, browse and snack.

DISTANCE: 1.6 miles (2.5km) **ALLOW:** 3–6 hours

START

DARTMOUTH STREET
➕ G7 🚇 Back Bay Station

1 From Back Bay Station, walk several blocks down Dartmouth Street, crossing Columbus Avenue, taking note of the brick sidewalks and brownstone buildings on Chandler and Appleton streets.

2 Continue down Dartmouth to Tremont Street and turn left. On the left are the Boston Center for the Arts (▷ 82) and jazz supper club The Beehive (▷ 84).

3 Across Tremont, find much-loved restaurants such as B&G Oysters and The Butcher Shop (▷ 84).

4 From The Butcher Shop, take a left, returning down Tremont and pass gift shops and bistros such as Aquitaine and Metropolis.

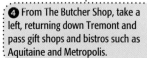

END

MASSACHUSETTS AVENUE
➕ F8 🚇 Massachusetts Avenue

8 Walk three blocks past Columbus Avenue and follow South End mall, a flower-filled walkway to the left, until it meets Massachusetts Avenue.

7 You're now in the South End's trendiest section, full of restaurants, galleries and stores. Return on Washington, passing restaurants such as The Gallows (▷ 84), and stores like Lekker Home. Next take a right on West Concord Street.

6 Continue down West Brookline, passing Blackstone Square, a small neighborhood park. When you reach Washington Street, take a left.

5 Where Tremont crosses West Brookline Street, take a left.

BACK BAY AND THE SOUTH END WALK

Shopping

ALAN BILZERIAN

alanbilzerian.com

This high-end shop is a fun one for window-shopping for the latest clothes from Rick Owens, Yohji Yamamoto and other big-name designers.

✚ H6 ✉ 34 Newbury Street ☎ 617/536-1001 🚇 Arlington

ALLEN EDMONDS

allenedmonds.com

These American-made handcrafted shoes are meticulously made. They also sell bags, belts and other sundry items.

✚ H6 ✉ 36 Newbury Street ☎ 617/247-3363 🚇 Arlington

BARNEYS NEW YORK

barneys.com

A second home to the city's high-spending hipsters, where you can find of-the-moment labels such as 3.1 by Phillip Lim and Lanvin. Don't miss the luxurious shoe section.

✚ G7 ✉ 100 Huntington Avenue 🚇 617/385-3300 🚇 Copley

BEAD + FIBER

beadandfiber.net

With its array of yarns and beads, this colorful shop is an inspiration for artists and beginners alike. Very lively during the SOWA Artists Guild First Fridays (5–9, year round).

✚ J8 ✉ 460 Harrison Avenue ☎ 617/426-2323 🚇 Back Bay/South End

CRUSH BOUTIQUE

shopcrushboutique.com

This store offers temptation after temptation from tops, sweaters and sequined mini-dresses to fun jewelry, denim and tailored jackets.

✚ F6 ✉ 264 Newbury Street ☎ 617/424-0010 🚇 Hynes

FLOCK BOUTIQUE

flockboston.com

This store concentrates on informal youthful styles with easy-to-wear clothes: from dresses and sweaters to hats, fingerless mittens, unusual shoes and jewelry.

✚ H8 ✉ 274 Shawmut Avenue ☎ 617/391-0222 🚇 Back Bay

GIFTED

madebymarie.com

As well as creating her own jewelry, pottery and photographs, Marie Corcoran shares her crafts store with local talent. Find fun baby clothes alongside sophisticated silk ties.

✚ H8 ✉ 2 Dartmouth Street ☎ 617/716-9924 🚇 Back Bay

GOORIN BROS

goorin.com

If you like hats, you'll love Goorin Bros, which has hats for men, for women, for work and play, and for kids. You'll find everything from fedoras to flat caps.

✚ G6 ✉ 130 Newbury Street 🚇 617/247-4287 🚇 Copley

LIFE IS GOOD

lifeisgood.com

Guilt-free shopping with ten percent of profits going to help children in need. Choose from a good selection of casual and comfortable clothing, bags, socks, hats and more branded with the Life Is Good logo.

✚ F6 ✉ 285 Newbury Street ☎ 617/262-5068 🚇 Hynes

LUCKY BRAND

luckybrand.com

Known for its high-quality jeans, Lucky Brand also produces good-quality casual wear as well as sportswear, activewear,

underwear, accessories and fragrance for men, women and children.

➕ G6 ✉ 2 Copley Place ☎ 617/247-1289 🚇 Copley

MODELL'S SPORTING GOODS

modells.com

This family-owned shop sells athletic equipment, footwear and apparel. It's also got replica jerseys for sports fans.

➕ H6 ✉ 480 Boylston Street ☎ 617/236-7234

NEWBURY COMICS

newburycomics.com

Started 40 years ago by two MIT college students, this iconic store sells comics, records, CDs and all sorts of pop culture items.

➕ G6 ✉ 332 Newbury Street ☎ 617/236-4930 🚇 Hynes Convention Center

THE NORTH FACE

thenorthface.com

This well-established company sells quality performance apparel, equipment and footwear for those who love the great outdoors.

➕ G6 ✉ 326 Newbury Street ☎ 617/536-8060

PRUDENTIAL CENTER

prudentialcenter.com

This shopping, dining and entertainment complex has a dozen clothes stores to choose from, including Chico's, Ann Taylor, J.Jill and Olympia Sports. There are also shoe and accessories shops, gift and specialty stores (such as Cranes stationery) and a hardware store. Those looking for homeware and soft furnishings can head to Saks Fifth Avenue and Lord & Taylor. Other facilities include a post office, ATMs, a food court and full-sevice restaurants such as

Legal Sea Foods and L'Espalier, so you can easily spend hours here.

➕ G7 ✉ Between Boylston Street and Huntington Avenue 🚇 Prudential

SIMON PEARCE

simonpearce.com

Simon Pearce is a well-known New England artist, making exquisite art glass and utilitarian glassware beautiful enough to be decorative pieces. Other homeware items such as crockery, vases and lampshades are also available.

➕ G6 ✉ 103 Newbury Street ☎ 617/450-8388 🚇 Arlington

WILLIAMS-SONOMA

williams-sonoma.com

For the cook who has everything—or so you thought until you came in here: from Dualit toasters and heart-shaped muffin baking trays to top-quality linens.

➕ G7 ✉ Copley Place ☎ 617/262-3080 🚇 Copley

VINEYARD VINES

vineyardvines.com

Vineyard Vines, a local company famous for its fun neckties and smiling pink whale logo. It stocks clothing and accessories for men, women and children.

➕ G7 ✉ Copley Place ☎ 617/960-5063 🚇 Copley

INDEPENDENT SHOPS

How to best to find homegrown and family-run boutiques and specialty shops? When walking on Newbury Street, look up. The second, third and fourth floors of the street's Victorian brownstone buildings are favorite spaces for those with less money to burn on front-and-center retail space, but with plenty of interesting and unique wares to sell.

Entertainment and Nightlife

BERKLEE PERFORMANCE CENTER

berklee.edu/bpc

This Back Bay venue seats 1,220 and hosts jazz, pop, folk and world music concerts by international performers and by the students and staff of the Berklee College of Music.

F7 136 Massachusetts Avenue 617/747–2261 Hynes Convention Center

BLEACHER BAR

bleacherbarboston.com

The ultimate sports bar inside Fenway Park's Green Monster. Small and busy at game time, the field-level view looks right across centerfield to home plate.

E7 82 Lansdowne Street 617/262-2424 Kenmore

BOSTON BEER WORKS

beerworks.net

Sports bar and micro-brewery with handcrafted ales, lagers, stouts and pilsners on tap, and serving upscale bar food. Located near Fenway Park, so expect crowds on game days. Brewery tours and tastings available.

E7 61 Brookline Avenue 617/536-2337 Kenmore

BOSTON CENTER FOR THE ARTS

bcaonline.org

Three stages at this South End performance space house several contemporary theater companies, including the provocative Company One and the cutting-edge SpeakEasy Stage Company.

H7 539 Tremont Street 617/426-5000 Back Bay Station

BUKOWSKI TAVERN

bukowskitavern.net

A great choice for beer lovers, with more than 100 varieties on offer at this friendly and unpretentious spot. Food is also served, think comforting chili dogs, burgers and mac 'n' cheese.

F7 50 Dalton Street 617/437-9999 Hynes Convention Center

CASK 'N FLAGON

casknflagon.com

The perfect pit-stop before, during and after a Red Sox game, this rowdy sports bar has big-screen TVs galore.

D7 62 Brookline Avenue 617/536-4840 Kenmore

CITY BAR

citybarboston.com

Ultra-dim lighting and a stellar martini list make this intimate little gathering place inside the Lenox Hotel perfect for a nightcap or a mysterious rendezvous.

G6 65 Exeter Street 617/933-4800 Copley, Back Bay Station

CLUB CAFÉ

clubcafe.com

A nightly playground for the GLBTQ community, this lounge, restaurant and "video bar" has something for everyone.

H7 209 Columbus Avenue 617/536-0966 Back Bay Station

DELUX CAFE

thedelux.com

Christmas lights, Elvis statues and Dr. Seuss wallpaper in the bathrooms make this a fun spot to check out. The interior

---

BLUE LAWS

Most bars in Boston and Cambridge close at 1am during the week, and 2am on the weekends—though you may find restaurants in Chinatown that serve later. Happy-hour specials, such as 2-for-1 drinks, are prohibited, though some bars serve free appetizers after work.

here is as eclectic as its clientele. Make an evening of it and sample the tasty bar menu.

H7 ✉ 100 Chandler Street ☎ 617/338-5258 🚇 Back Bay Station

FRANKLIN CAFÉ

franklincafe.com

Open very late, this busy restaurant is where chefs hang out after work. The home-cured corned beef and cabbage, and whole roast chicken, are legendary. The bar serves wines, cocktails and local micro-brews. No reservations.

H8 ✉ 278 Shawmut Avenue ☎ 617/350-0010 🚇 Back Bay

HATCH SHELL

hatchshell.com

The Boston Pops Orchestra gives free concerts here in early July. The highlight is the concert with fireworks on July 4. Other musical groups perform throughout the summer.

H5 ✉ Esplanade, Embankment Road ☎ 617/626-4970 🚇 Charles/MGH, Arlington

HOUSE OF BLUES BOSTON

houseofblues.com

With its combination of lounge, theater and restaurant and live blues, gospel, jazz and rock shows, the House of Blues wears many hats.

E7 ✉ 15 Lansdowne Street ☎ 888/693-2583 🚇 Kenmore

HUNTINGTON THEATRE COMPANY

huntingtontheatre.org

Performances from Boston University's resident professional troupe include European and American, classical and modern, comedies and musicals.

F7 ✉ 264 Huntington Avenue ☎ 617/266-0800 🚇 Symphony

JORDAN HALL

necmusic.edu

This glittering and acoustically perfect venue, in the prestigious New England Conservatory, showcases the resident Boston Philharmonic, Boston Baroque and Cantata Singers. Conservatory students perform free concerts year-round.

E8 ✉ 30 Gainsborough Street, one block west of Symphony Hall ☎ 617/585-1260 🚇 Symphony

LUCKY STRIKE

jilliansboston.com

Three floors of fun pack in the crowds at Lucky Strike, where activities include bowling, 150 high-tech games, pool, shuffleboard and more. A full restaurant and brewery are also on site.

E7 ✉ 145 Ipswich Street ☎ 617/437-0300 🕐 Daily 12–2am 🚇 Kenmore

PUPPET SHOWPLACE THEATER

puppetshowplace.org

Masters of pantomime spin yarns with surprisingly elaborate puppets that draw on traditions from around the world.

F7 ✉ 32 Station Street, Brookline ☎ 617/731-6400

SYMPHONY HALL

bso.org

"Symphony" is home to the Boston Symphony Orchestra from Sep–May. The orchestra often performs on Friday afternoon, Saturday, Tuesday and Thursday evenings. Call for the current schedule, as performance days vary from month-to-month. The Boston Pops Orchestra concerts are held here in December, May and June before moving to the Hatch Shell (▷ left) in July.

F7 ✉ 301 Massachusetts Avenue ☎ Box office 617/266-1200; general information 617/266-1492 🚇 Symphony

Where to Eat

THE BEEHIVE ($$)

beehiveboston.com

This fun supper club serves an eclectic menu and free nightly entertainment ranging from jazz to rock and roll. The weekend jazz brunch is wildly popular so make reservations ahead of time.

➕ H7 ✉ 541 Tremont Street, South End ☎ 617/423-0069 🕐 Dinner daily, brunch Sat–Sun 🚇 Back Bay Station

THE BUTCHER SHOP ($$$)

thebutchershopboston.com

Meat, meat and more meat is king at this South End butcher/wine bar/restaurant. Choose from their own pâtés and sausages, great steaks and charcuterie.

➕ H7 ✉ 552 Tremont Street ☎ 617/423-4800 🕐 Sun–Wed 11.30–10, Thu–Sat 11.30–11 🚇 Back Bay Station

CASA ROMERO ($$)

casaromero.com

Consistently winning rave reviews for authentic Mexican cuisine, this cozy spot down an alley is a standout.

➕ F6 ✉ 30 Gloucester St ☎ 617/536-4341 🕐 Dinner daily 🚇 Hynes Convention Center

EATALY ($$)

eataly.com

Eataly Boston, part of the enormous Italian food emporium, offers everything from a market to pushcarts to sit-down restaurants. Shop, snack, drink and browse at this three-story wonderland of Italian specialties.

➕ G7 ✉ 800 Boylston Street ☎ 617/536-0770 🕐 Mon–Fri 7–11, Sat–Sun 9–11 🚇 Prudential

FLOUR BAKERY ($)

flourbakery.com

Grab melt-in-the-mouth breakfasts, lunches and dinners (plus delicious pies, cakes, pastries and cookies) at this neighborhood favorite.

➕ H8 ✉ 1595 Washington Street ☎ 617/267-4300 🚇 Back Bay/South End

THE GALLOWS ($$)

thegallowsboston.com

A loud and fun neighborhood bar, The Gallows is a favorite of the locals who like its casual atmosphere and somewhat quirky comfort-food menu.

➕ Off map at G9 ✉ 1395 Washington Street ☎ 617/425-0200 🕐 Lunch Mon–Fir, dinner daily, brunch Sat–Sun 🚇 Back Bay Station

PETIT ROBERT BISTRO ($$)

petitrobertbistro.com

A delightful, and very authentic, Parisian cafe, Petit Robert offers classic French fare with excellent service. This is the place to go when craving something classic and exquisite such as *coq au vin* or *escargots*.

➕ E6 ✉ 480 Columbus Avenue ☎ 617/867-0600 🕐 Lunch, dinner daily, brunch Sat–Sun 🚇 Mass Ave

SELECT OYSTER BAR ($$$)

selectboston.com

This excellent seafood bar is a sleek, sexy spot to enjoy all sorts of fresh seafood, not just oysters. In a nice departure from a lobster roll, the Maine lobster salad is outstanding.

➕ F6 ✉ 50 Gloucester Street, Back Bay ☎ 857/239-8064 🕐 Lunch, dinner daily 🚇 Hynes Convention Center

This historic and multicultural city across the river from Boston is one of America's greatest academic centers, thanks to universities such as Harvard and the Massachusetts Institute of Technology.

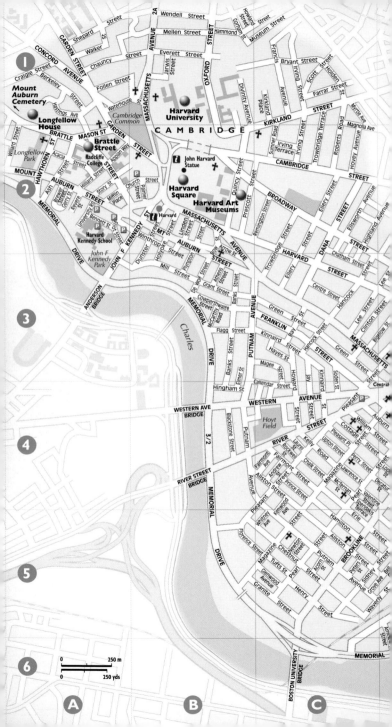

Cambridge

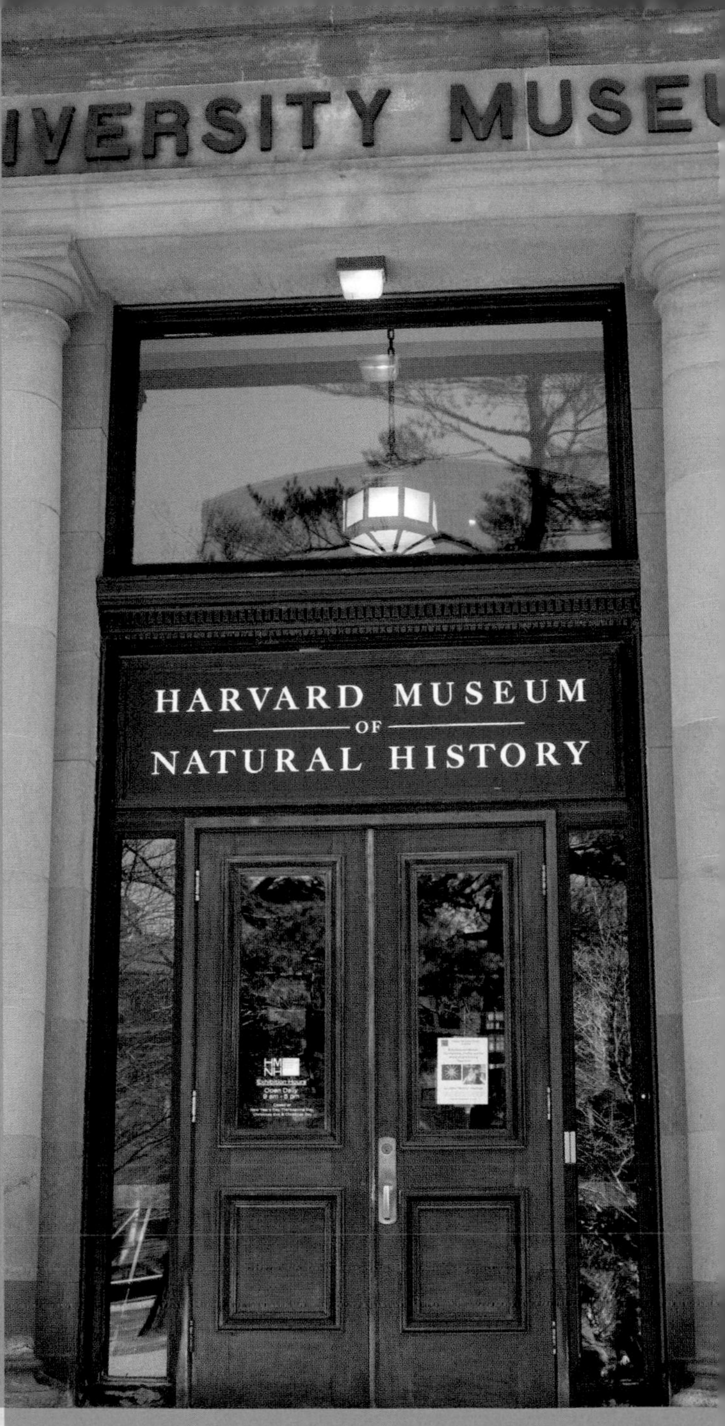
HARVARD MUSEUM
OF
NATURAL HISTORY

Harvard Art Museums

Few universities have such an enviable, world-class collection of museums.

The Harvard Art Museums Uniting all of the museums is a stunning glass roof, designed by Italian architect Renzo Piano. Within, the galleries have distinctive spaces for their respective permanent collections. The Fogg is known for its comprehensive collection of Western European art (Italian early Renaissance, 17th-century Dutch and 19th-century French and British paintings), the Busch-Reisinger for art from German-speaking countries (from Klee and Kandinsky to Anselm Kiefer and Gerhard Richter), while the Arthur M. Sackler's collections of Asian art, ancient Mediterranean and Byzantine works, and Indian and Islamic art are world-renowned. With its glass roof, the stunning Calderwood Courtyard is a jaw-dropping example of modern architecture.

Harvard Museum of Natural History (HMNH) More than 4,000 models of 830 plant species, in the Blaschka Glass Flowers exhibit are so realistic you cannot believe they are made of glass. Elsewhere are wild animals and birds, plus rocks and minerals, including precious gems.

Peabody Museum This is one of the world's finest collections recording human culture. The detailed historical and cultural backgrounds given for the Native American people is particularly interesting.

THE BASICS

harvard.edu/museums

⊞ B2

✉ Harvard Art Museums: 32 Quincy Street. HMNH: 26 Oxford Street. Peabody: 11 Divinity Avenue

☎ Art museums: 617/495-9400. HMNH: 617/495-3045. Peabody: 617/496-1027

🕐 Art museums: Daily 10–5. HMNH and Peabody: Daily 9–5

♿ Very good

💵 Moderate. Only one ticket is needed to visit both the HMNH and the Peabody. CityPass applies

HIGHLIGHTS

● Impressionists (Fogg)
● Jade (Sackler)
● Glass flowers (HMNH)
● Native American exhibits (Peabody)

Harvard Square and Harvard University

HIGHLIGHTS

● Harvard Yard
● Excellent museums
● Browsing in a bookshop all evening

TIPS

● You'll learn a lot on a guided tour of Harvard. Stop in the Holyoke Arcade at 1350 Massachusetts Avenue to sign up for a free tour.
● Stroll down to the river to watch the rowing crews practice.

One of the most significant strands in the fabric of Bostonian life is the academic scene. In Cambridge you can walk through hallowed Harvard Yard in the footsteps of the great, then take time to enjoy Harvard Square.

Harvard University Among the first things the Massachusetts Bay colonists did was provide for the training of ministers, and thus was founded, in 1636, one of the world's most respected seats of learning. Most of its historic buildings are in Harvard Yard, entered across the street from the First Parish Church. Ahead, in front of Bulfinch's University Hall, is a statue by Daniel Chester French of benefactor John Harvard. The elegant 18th-century redbrick halls grouped around this, the Old Yard, are dormitories.

Clockwise from left: A café in Harvard Square; students gather around the ornate gateway to a Harvard college; students on lawns outside Widener Memorial Library; a street musician entertains in Harvard Square; New Yard in the fall; pedestrians and students mingle in Harvard Square

Behind University Hall is New Yard, with Memorial Church on the left facing the pillared facade of Widener Library. Pass beside H.H. Richardson's Sever Hall to emerge in Quincy Street opposite the Carpenter Center for the Visual Arts, the only Le Corbusier building in North America. The Harvard Art Museums (▷ 88–89) are next door. Radcliffe Institute is alongside Cambridge Common, around the lovely Radcliffe Yard.

Harvard Square The newsstand by the T is a famous landmark (▷ 95) in this "square," which is actually more of a district. Here you can watch chess games, listen to street musicians, sit in an outdoor café, shop for clothes and books, or in the evening you can go to a club for jazz or reggae.

THE BASICS

harvard.edu

➕ B1/B2

✉ Harvard University: Harvard Yard, Peabody Street

📺 City of Cambridge Visitor Information Booth: 617/497-1630; University: 617/495-1573

🕐 Daily

🍴 Plenty nearby

Ⓗ Harvard

💲 Free

❓ Campus tours Mon–Sat, check on-line for schedule.

More to See

LONGFELLOW HOUSE AND BRATTLE STREET

nps.gov/long

In the pre-Revolutionary 1770s the land on either side of Brattle Street was owned by loyalist families, forced to quit when the Patriots took over the area in 1774. Henry Wadsworth Longfellow came to No. 105 Brattle Street as a lodger in 1837 and wrote many of his poems here. The historic gardens are open year-round and have no admission fee.

➕ A1/A2 ✉ 105 Brattle Street ☎ 617/ 876-4492 🕐 Late May–late Oct. Check for hours 🚇 Harvard, then pleasant walk (0.5 miles/0.8km) 💷 Inexpensive

MIT BUILDINGS

web.mit.edu

MIT has some impressive modern architecture. You are free to wander around the campus. Seek out Eero Saarinen's serene round chapel (1955). Don't miss Frank Gehry's whimsical Ray and Maria Stata Center for Computer, Information and Intelligence Sciences, on Vassar Street. On and near Ames Street the low Wiesner and the tall Green buildings are the work of I.M. Pei.

➕ E4 ✉ Massachusetts Avenue, Vassar Street, Ames Street 🚇 Kendall 💷 Free

MIT SCULPTURES

On the campus are two Henry Moore reclining figure pieces (1963, 1976), Alexander Calder's black steel *The Big Sail* (1965) and Michael Heizer's pink granite *Guennette* (1977).

➕ E5 ✉ Memorial Drive 🕐 Daily 🚇 Kendall 💷 Free

MOUNT AUBURN CEMETERY

A little out of the way, but a beautiful place. It was founded in 1831 as the country's first rural garden cemetery and is still very popular with bird and plant lovers. Longfellow now rests here, as does the artist Winslow Homer.

➕ Off map at A1 ✉ 580 Mount Auburn Street ☎ 617/547-7105 🕐 Daily 🚇 Harvard, then walk or Watertown bus

Mount Auburn Cemetery

Portrait of Henry Wadsworth Longfellow

Harvard Square

Cambridge, compact with noteworthy institutions, makes an excellent walk, dotted with history, entertainment and shops.

DISTANCE: 1 mile (1.6km) **ALLOW:** 3–4 hours

START

JOHN HARVARD STATUE, HARVARD YARD (▷ 90) ✚ B2 🚇 Harvard

END

CAMBRIDGE COMMON (▷ 91) ✚ B2 🚇 Harvard

❶ Begin on the Harvard University Green, on the site of the country's oldest college. Walk out of the gates and cross Massachusetts Avenue.

❽ Follow Massachusetts Avenue up to Cambridge Common, a magnet for students and professors looking to relax.

❷ Go straight down Church Street, passing numerous shops, until Church hits Brattle Street (▷ 92). Take a right on Brattle.

❼ Step into The Coop (▷ 94), Harvard's renowned bookstore, where you can browse to your heart's content. If you need a break, The Coop has a cafe where you can recharge. Return to Massachusetts Avenue and turn left.

❸ Continue down Brattle Street, passing stately mansions, on the way to the Longfellow House (▷ 92), where Henry Wadsworth Longfellow once lived.

❻ Farther up, pass the Brattle Theatre (▷ 96), an independent cinema and one of the Square's most revered cultural stops. Follow Brattle to the left, where it meets up with Massachusetts Avenue.

❹ Turn around on Brattle and head back toward Harvard Square, passing the American Repertory Theater (▷ 96) on the way.

❺ In the last blocks of Brattle, duck into the row's unique stores and gift shops.

Shopping

ABODEON

abodeon.com

Enjoy a stockpile of modern and retro housewares in this store. The vintage furniture is particularly impressive, but you may also want to pick up a few pieces of tableware while you're at it.

➕ Off map at B1 ✉ 1731 Massachusetts Avenue ☎ 617/497-0137 🚇 Harvard

CABOT'S CANDY

cabotscandy.com

Cabot's has been in business since 1927, when it started out selling hand-pulled saltwater taffy. Today, you'll find taffy, as well as all sorts of other delicious confections, like fudge and brittle.

➕ B2 ✉ 1300 Massachusetts Ave ☎ 617/497-7500 🚇 Havard

CAMBRIDGE ANTIQUE MARKET

marketantique.com

A fantastic Cambridge cooperative with dealers selling china, glass, quilts, clothes, silver, jewelry and collectibles.

➕ Off map at G3 ✉ 201 Monsignor O'Brien Highway, diagonally opposite the Lechmere T ☎ 617/868-9655 🚇 Lechmere

CAMBRIDGE ARTISTS' COOPERATIVE

cambridgeartistscoop.com

This artist-owned and operated coop operates the Gallery of Contemporary American Craft, showcasing the work of more than 200 artists from across the country. Shop for everything from ceramics to jewelry to fiber arts.

➕ B2 ✉ 59a Church Street ☎ 617/868-4434 🚇 Harvard

CARDULLO'S

cardullos.com

Crammed with specialty foods and first-rate baked goods, this family-run deli is the place to pick up all your favorite foods and ingredients.

➕ A2 ✉ 6 Brattle Street ☎ 617/491-8888 🚇 Harvard

HARVARD BOOK STORE

harvard.com

Since 1932, this independent shop has sold academic titles, as well as new and used fiction and non-fiction titles.

➕ B2 ✉ 1256 Massachusetts Avenue ☎ 617/661-1515 🚇 Harvard

THE HARVARD COOP

thecoop.com

With its official Harvard logo clothing and gifts, The Coop is much more than a 130-year-old student store. There are four floors of books and dorm furnishings, plus a fun café.

➕ B2 ✉ 1400 Massachusetts Avenue ☎ 617/499-2000 🚇 Harvard

HARVARD SQUARE

harvardsquare.com

Cambridge's Harvard Square is a maze of streets with bookshops, music shops and clothes stores, much of it geared toward students. There's a wide variety of restaurants and cafés. Check out Brattle Street, Church Street, Eliot Street (with the Charles Square complex just off), JFK Street and Dunster Street. As the bigger chains have moved into the area, so some of the smaller local shops have moved, or opened up, just north of Harvard and there's now a clutch of

---

BOOKSTORES

Cambridge, and Harvard Square in particular, has an amazing concentration of independent bookshops. Pick up a complete guide from the information kiosk by Harvard Square T.

good independant clothes and gift shops on Massachusetts Avenue.
🕂 B2

HENRY BEAR'S PARK

henrybear.com

A well-established store that is just what you'd want and expect from a great toy shop. It frequently wins awards for its first-class, imaginative playthings.
🕂 C2 ✉ 17 White Street ☎ 617/547-8424
🚇 Porter Square

JOIE DE VIVRE

joiedevivre.net

Selling toys for all ages, this fun store offers everything from wind-up toys and singing animals to kaleidoscopes, snow-globes and music boxes.
🕂 Off map at A1 ✉ 1792 Massachusetts Avenue ☎ 617/864-8188 🚇 Porter Square

LEAVITT & PEIRCE INC.

leavitt-peirce.com

Since 1883, this tobacco shop has been a fixture in the area, peddling bins of tobacco, pipes, men's shaving supplies and vintage chess sets.
🕂 B2 ✉ 1316 Massachusetts Avenue
☎ 617/547-0576 🚇 Harvard

MINT JULEP

shopmintjulep.com

Attractive, stylish, but accessible and timeless clothing in luscious fabrics and colors are the style here. The accessories are equally well chosen.
🕂 B2 ✉ 6 Church Street ☎ 617/576-6468
🚇 Harvard

OUT OF TOWN NEWS

This iconic newsstand might be one of the most recognizable sights in Harvard Square. It sells newspapers and magazines from around the world. And while

the world may be mostly digital, it has managed to remain a beloved fixture.
🕂 B2 ✉ Harvard Square ☎ 617/354–1441
🚇 Harvard Square Station

SCHOENHOF'S FOREIGN BOOKS

schoenhofs.com

For more than 150 years Schoenhof's has offered foreign-language books, including classics in original Greek or Latin, contemporary literature, philosophy, children's books, poetry and language materials. French, German, Italian and Spanish titles are featured, with hundreds of other languages too.
🕂 B2 ✉ 76A Mount Auburn Street
☎ 617/547-8855 🚇 Harvard

TESS & CARLOS

tessandcarlos.com

Stylish, classic clothes, shoes and accessories for men and women. The cashmere sweater collection and clothing by Italian designers are impressive.
🕂 A2 ✉ 20 Brattle Street ☎ 617/864-8377
🚇 Harvard

THE WORLD'S ONLY CURIOUS GEORGE STORE

thecuriousgeorgestore.com

This awesome bookstore is certainly devoted to the famous monkey, but it also has a wonderful selection of children's books of all types.
🕂 B2 ✉ 1 JFK Street ☎ 617/498-0062
🚇 Harvard

OUTLETS CENTRAL

The outlets at Assembly Row (assemblyrow.com) in Somerville are part of an ambitious development. As well as a new Orange line T-stop (Assembly), there are 50 premier outlet stores and New England's only LEGOLAND Discovery Center.

Entertainment and Nightlife

AMERICAN REPERTORY THEATER

amrep.org

A highly regarded professional repertory company, staging classical and often groundbreaking original drama.

🏠 A2 ✉ Loeb Drama Center, 64 Brattle Street
☎ 617/547-8300 🚇 Harvard

BRATTLE THEATRE

brattlefilm.org

Vintage films and film festivals attract fans to this small, one-screen theater. It's best to buy tickets online for popular screenings.

🏠 A2 ✉ 40 Brattle Street ☎ 617/876-6837
🚇 Harvard

CANTAB LOUNGE

cantab-lounge.com

Neighborhood gathering spot, bar and grill, Cantab offers two venues with nightly performances of an eclectic variety of music and spoken word events. Monday night is Open Mic night.

🏠 C3 ✉ 738 Massachusetts Avenue
☎ 617/354-2685 🚇 Central

CLUB PASSIM

clubpassim.com

The Cambridge area's premier folk music venue attracts both up-and-coming and established performers.

🏠 B2 ✉ 47 Palmer Street ☎ 617/492-7679
🚇 Harvard

GREEN STREET

greenstreetgrill.com

Varied menu featuring seasonal entrées in a comfortable atmosphere. The cocktail menu is extensive, with fine wines and craft beers that make this neighborhood fixture a popular place to drink.

🏠 D4 ✉ 280 Green Street ☎ 617/876-1655
🕐 Dinner daily from 5.30pm 🚇 Central, then short walk

HARVARD FILM ARCHIVE

hcl.harvard.edu/hfa

The Film Archive offers showings of cult and independent films at Harvard's Carpenter Center for the Visual Arts.

🏠 B2 ✉ 24 Quincy Street ☎ 617/495-4700
🚇 Harvard

HASTY PUDDING THEATER

hastypudding.org

Home to the touring Hasty Pudding Theatricals company and to the American Repertory Theater's annual "New Stages" series of contemporary productions.

🏠 B2 ✉ 12 Holyoke Street ☎ 617/495-5205
🚇 Harvard

JOSÉ MATEO'S BALLET THEATRE

ballettheatre.org

Directed by José Mateo, this notable professional company performs a community-friendly mix of classical and contemporary ballet.

🏠 B2 ✉ 400 Harvard Street ☎ 617/354-7467
🚇 Harvard

THE MIDDLE EAST

mideastclub.com

The premier venue for alternative rock for not only Cambridge, but also Boston. The Middle East has three rooms for performers—upstairs, downstairs and in the restaurant.

🏠 C3 ✉ 472/480 Massachusetts Avenue
☎ 617/864-3278 🚇 Central

NOIR BAR

noir-bar.com

Sophisticated and sultry, this popular nook in the Charles Hotel provides comfortable couches for a late-night (2am) martini or seasonal cocktail.

🏠 B2 ✉ 1 Bennett Street ☎ 617/661-8010
🚇 Harvard

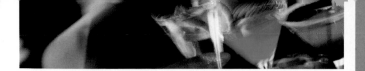

REGATTABAR

regattabarjazz.com

First-class jazz acts come to Harvard Square at this classy bar in The Charles Hotel.

🞣 A2 ✉ 1 Bennett Street ☎ 617/661-5000 🕑 Closed Mon 🚇 Harvard

RYLES

rylesjazz.com

The emphasis here in Inman Square is on Latin jazz, with food downstairs. There is a weekly learn-to-salsa Latin dance night.

🞣 E3 ✉ 212 Hampshire Street ☎ 617/876-9330 🕑 Music: Tue–Sun from 8.30pm, Sun jazz brunch: 10–3 🚇 Central, then long walk or bus 83; Harvard, then bus 69 along Cambridge Street

SANDERS THEATRE

fas.harvard.edu

A 1,600-seat neo-Gothic theater at Harvard, that showcases classical and world music. Despite its size the 180-degree stage design allows an imtimate feel.

🞣 B2 ✉ Quincy Street at Cambridge Street ☎ 617/496-2222 🚇 Harvard

SCULLERS JAZZ CLUB

SkullersJazz.com

Located in the DoubleTree Suites hotel, this boasts a roll call of greats over the years, from Diana Krall and Norah Jones to Michael Bublé and Jamie Cullum.

🞣 B4 ✉ 400 Soldiers Field Road ☎ 617/562-1111 🚇 Central

Where to Eat

PRICES
Prices are approximate, based on a 3-course meal for one person.
$$$ over $40
$$ $20–$40
$ under $20

BONDIR ($$$)

bondircambridge.com

Award-winning chef Jason Bond presents only the freshest foods at his farmhouse-style restaurant, so the menu changes daily, and makes use of local ingredients wherever possible. Make sure to reserve a table, as the homey, 28-seat restaurant tends to fill up fast.

🞣 E3 ✉ 279A Broadway ☎ 617/661-0009 🕑 Wed–Sun 5pm–10pm 🚇 Central

BORDER CAFÉ ($)

bordercafe.com

Fun, friendly and crowded, this popular restaurant serves large portions of tasty Cajun and Tex-Mex favorites, including fajitas, tacos, jambalaya and margaritas. This is good option for families.

🞣 B2 ✉ 32 Church Street ☎ 617/864-6100 🕑 Lunch, dinner daily (till late) 🚇 Harvard

CHRISTINA'S ($)

christinasicecream.com

Christina's homemade ice cream and sorbet draw crowds. An ever-changing menu of flavors ranges from ordinary to unusual, such as burnt sugar, avocado, cardamom and bergamot and is always spectacular.

🞣 D2 ✉ 1255 Cambridge Street ☎ 617/492-7021 🕑 Daily 🚇 Harvard

CRAIGIE ON MAIN ($$$)

craigieonmain.com

The menu is so interesting and tempting that regulars opt for the "Chef's Whim" four- or six-course tasting menus offered on Sunday after 9pm. Dishes use only the freshest local ingredients.

🔳 D4 ✉ 853 Main Street ☎ 617/497-5511 🕐 Dinner daily, brunch Sun 🚇 Central

HENRIETTA'S TABLE ($$–$$$)

Found at the Charles Hotel, this beloved restaurant served up farm-to-table food before it was ever a trend. With its focus on New England's cuisine, it's a favorite with locals and visitors alike.

🔳 B2 ✉ 1 Bennett Street ☎ 617/661-5005 🕐 Breakfast daily, lunch Mon–Fri, brunch, supper Sat–Sun 🚇 Harvard

HI-RISE ($)

While anything pastry-related here is excellent, Hi-Rise also offers hearty soups, sandwiches and more, making it a perfect pit stop for lunch.

🔳 B1 ✉ 1663 Massachusetts Avenue ☎ 617/492-3003 🕐 Mon–Fri 8–8, Sat–Sun 8–5 🚇 Harvard

L.A. BURDICK CHOCOLATE ($)

burdickchocolate.com

If heaven were a chocolate shop it might look something like this café. There's ample choice of pastries, cakes and hot drinks but surely it has be the chocolate "Harvard Square."

🔳 A2 ✉ 52 Brattle Street ☎ 617/491-4340 🕐 Daily 🚇 Harvard

LEGAL SEA FOODS ($$)

legalseafoods.com

Locally owned, Legal's serves up a wide range of fresh, no-fuss seafood to wide acclaim. The menu includes a handful of meat dishes and a decent kids menu for those traveling with little ones.

🔳 F4 ✉ 5 Cambridge Center, Kendall Square ☎ 617/864-3400 🕐 Lunch, dinner daily 🚇 Kendall

MR. BARTLEY'S BURGER COTTAGE ($)

Choose from more than two dozen burgers with sweet potato fries, plus salads, sandwiches and desserts.

🔳 B2 ✉ 1246 Massachusetts Avenue ☎ 617/354-6559 🕐 Lunch, dinner Mon–Sat. Closed Sun 🚇 Harvard

OLEANA ($$–$$$)

oleanarestaurant.com

Ana Sortun's innovative cuisine, based on eastern Mediterranean tradition, makes her one of New England's leading chefs. Using her husband's organic vegetables, she creates healthy and delicately spiced dishes.

🔳 E3 ✉ 134 Hampshire Street ☎ 617/661-0505 🕐 Dinner nightly from 5.30 🚇 Central

PARK ($$)

parkcambridge.com

With its armchairs and sofas, this lively neighborhood favorite serves a tempting mix of contemporary European and American dishes late into the night.

🔳 B2 ✉ 59 JFK Street ☎ 617/491-9851 🕐 Mon–Wed 5pm–1am, Thu–Sat 5pm–2am, Sun 10am–1am 🚇 Harvard

RUSSELL HOUSE TAVERN ($$)

russellhousecambridge.com

This welcoming tavern is a comfortable place to enjoy classic American fare that is elevated by excellent ingredients. The craft beer menu has interesting options.

🔳 A2 ✉ 14 JFK Street ☎ 617/500-3055 🕐 Lunch Mon–Fri, dinner daily, brunch Sat–Sun 🚇 Harvard

You could easily spend weeks in Boston and not come to the end of all the city has to offer. Dozens of historical and cultural attractions lie within easy day-trip reach and are worth exploring in their own right.

EAST
SOMERVILLE

28

SOMERVILLE

2A

CAMBRIDGE

CAMBRIDGE   STREET

MONSIGNOR

3   2

SOLDIERS   FIELD   ROAD

MASSACHUSETTS   AVENUE

EAST
CAMBRIDGE

ALLSTON

90

20

MEMORIAL   DRIVE

Charles   River   Basin

30

COMMONWEALTH   AVENUE

JFK National
Historic Site

BACK   BAY

BEACON   STREET

COOLIDGE
CORNER

LONGWOOD

Back Bay
Fens

2

HUNTINGTON   AVENUE

BROOKLINE
VILLAGE

BROOKLINE
HILL

ROXBURY
CROSSING

9

BOYLSTON   STREET

Frederick Law Olmsted
National Historic Site

Olmsted
Park

COLUMBUS   AVENUE

MARTIN LUTHER KING JR BLVD

Jamaica
Pond

Larz
Anderson
Park

Larz Anderson
Auto Museum

WASHINGTON   STREET

SEAVER   STREET

Arnold
Arboretum

Franklin
Park Zoo

28

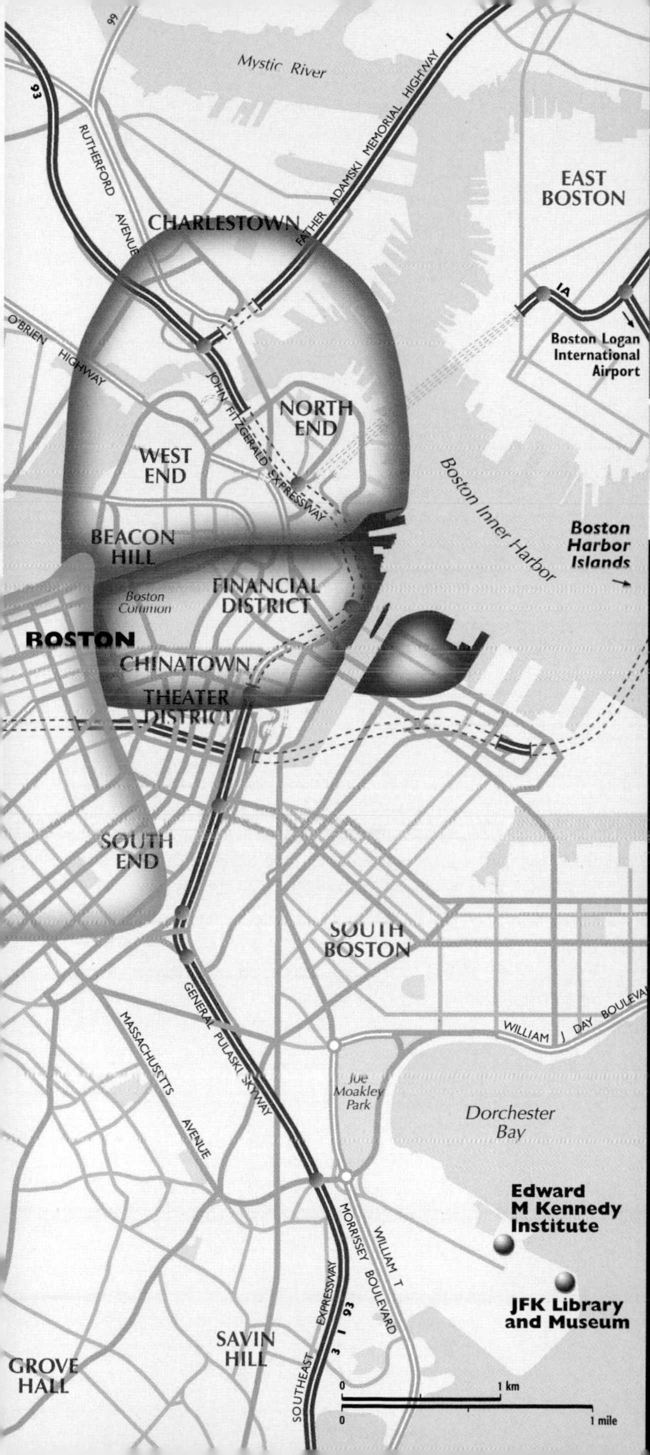

Mystic River

CHARLESTOWN

EAST BOSTON

RUTHERFORD AVENUE

FATHER ADAMSKI MEMORIAL HIGHWAY

95

93

O'BRIEN HIGHWAY

JOHN F FITZGERALD EXPRESSWAY

NORTH END

WEST END

BEACON HILL

Boston Common

FINANCIAL DISTRICT

1A

Boston Logan International Airport

Boston Inner Harbor

Boston Harbor Islands →

BOSTON

CHINATOWN

THEATER DISTRICT

SOUTH END

SOUTH BOSTON

WILLIAM J DAY BOULEVARD

MASSACHUSETTS AVENUE

GENERAL PULASKI SKYWAY

Joe Moakley Park

Dorchester Bay

MORRISSEY BOULEVARD

WILLIAM T

Edward M Kennedy Institute

JFK Library and Museum

SOUTHEAST EXPRESSWAY

3 93

GROVE HALL

SAVIN HILL

0   1 km

0   1 mile

Boston Harbor Islands

Peddocks Island in Boston Harbor

THE BASICS

bostonharborislands.org
nps.gov/boha/index.htm

🔲 See map ▷ 101

✉ Boston Harbor Islands Visitor Pavilion, 191 Atlantic Avenue

☎ 617/223-8666

🕐 Georges Island: May to mid-Oct daily ferries. The other islands: May–Labor Day daily

🍴 Cafés on Georges. Limited or drinking water on most islands. Take a picnic

🚢 Long Wharf, Quincy Shipyard and Logan Airport to Georges Island. Long Wharf and Quincy Shipyard to other islands. From Jun 1–Labor Day free water shuttles between islands

♿ Poor

💲 Ferry moderate. Water taxi free

❓ Organized activities and tours including lighthouse and occasional winter trips. Check websites for details

HIGHLIGHTS

● The sense of escape
● Picnicking on a beach
● Fort Warren's dungeons
● Views of Boston's skyline
● Bird-watching on all the islands

Gather wild raspberries, picnic on a beach, visit a ruined fort—all within sight of the city. These wildernesses are ringed by Boston, its airport and suburbs.

National Recreation Area Once defensive sites and home to prisons and poorhouses, the Boston Harbor Islands were largely ignored until they became a National Recreation Area in 1996.

Island hopping It's a 45-minute ferry ride from Long Wharf to Georges Island, and 20 minutes to Spectacle Island. From Georges water taxis loop to Lovells, Peddocks, Bumpkin and Grape. The islands are small, so you can visit more than one in a day, and each has its own character. Georges attracts most visitors. All have picnic areas (most have no fresh water so make sure you take bottled water). Take guided walks, hike trails on your own or just beachcomb (beaches are mostly pebbly). Lovells has a sandy, unsupervised swimming beach; Spectacle's sandy beach has lifeguards in summer.

Something for everyone On Georges clamber over Fort Warren (find the hidden spiral staircase and get superb views of the city). Peddocks and Lovells also have ruined forts. Bumpkin is where to pick raspberries. Join the hares on Lovells; study the wildlife in the rock pools, salt marsh and woodland on Peddocks; and on Grape, crunch along beaches covered in iridescent blue mussel shells.

TOP 25

JFK Library and Museum

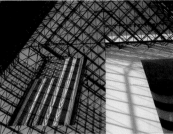

"A man may die, nations may rise and fall, but an idea lives on," said the late president John F. Kennedy, whose life, leadership and legacy are brilliantly evoked in this dramatic museum by the sea.

The setting The presidential library and its museum, constructed in 1979, are housed in an I.M. Pei building on Dorchester Bay, 4 miles (6.5km) southeast of downtown Boston. The building's two towers, of dark glass and smooth white concrete, command fine views of the city, the bay and Boston Harbor Islands. The lawns, dune grass and wild roses on the grounds recall the Kennedy summer home on Cape Cod.

The Museum An introductory film covers Kennedy's early years, from his childhood to the 1960 presidential campaign. Recreated settings include the White House corridors and the Oval Office, complete with the coconut inscribed "HELP" that led to his rescue after his naval ship sank in the Pacific. Videos cover significant events such as the Cuban Missile Crisis, space exploration and the assassination. Family photographs and exhibits cover the life and work of Jacqueline Kennedy Onassis.

The Presidential Library This is one of 14 presidential libraries holding the papers of 14 of the US presidents since Herbert Hoover. The Presidential Library System allows presidents to establish a library and museum.

THE BASICS

jfklibrary.org
✠ See map ▷ 101
✉ Columbia Point, Dorchester (Route 3/I-93 exit 15)
☎ 617/514-1600
🕐 Daily 9–5
🍴 Café on premises
Ⓙ JFK/U Mass, then free shuttle bus
♿ Excellent
💲 Moderate
🛈 Shop

HIGHLIGHTS

● The building, its setting and views
● Introductory video
● Oval Office
● Film and sound clips

TIP

● At the JFK Library, don't miss the Hemingway collection, which includes manuscripts and artifacts from the late, great writer.

More to See

ARNOLD ARBORETUM

arboretum.harvard.edu

Stunning in all seasons, this hilly park is part of the Emerald Necklace.

➕ See map ▷ 100 ✉ 125 Arborway, Jamaica Plain ☎ 617/524-1718 🕐 Daily dawn–dusk 🚇 Orange line to Forest Hills

EDWARD M. KENNEDY INSTITUTE

emkinstitute.org

Next door to the JFK Museum, this interactive museum has visitors see what it's like to be a U.S. Senator. Digital exhibits, replicas of the U.S. Senate Chamber and Senator Kennedy's Washington, D.C. Russell Senate office, are fascinating.

➕ See map ▷ 101 ✉ Columbia Point, Dorchester (Route 3/I-93 exit 15) ☎ 617/740-7000 🕐 Tues–Sun 10–5 💰 Moderate

FRANKLIN PARK ZOO

zoonewengland.org

Another link in the Emerald Necklace, the zoo features lion and tiger habitats, a Giraffe Savannah, and a 4-acre (1.6ha) mixed-species area called the Serengeti Crossing with zebras, ostriches and wildebeests. The Tropical Forest, with Western Lowland Gorilla environment, is quite popular.

➕ See map ▷ 100 ✉ 1 Franklin Park Road ☎ 617/541-5466 🕐 Daily 🍴 Café or picnic 🚇 Forest Hills, then bus 16 💰 Moderate

FREDERICK LAW OLMSTED NATIONAL HISTORIC SITE

nps.gov/frla

This famous landscape architect designed Boston Common, as well as Central Park and countless other green spaces in the U.S. Here you can tour the grounds and arrange weekend walking tours.

➕ See map ▷ 100 ✉ 99 Warren Street ☎ 617/566-1689 🕐 Daily 🚇 Brookline Hills (Green line D) then 0.75-mile (1.2km) walk 💰 Free

JFK NATIONAL HISTORIC SITE

Take a trip to Brookline and President Kennedy's boyhood home, filled with photographs and other memorabilia.

➕ A7 ✉ 83 Beals Street ☎ 617/566-7937 🕐 May–Oct Wed–Sun 9.30–5 🚇 Coolidge Corner (Green line C) 💰 Tour inexpensive

LARZ ANDERSON AUTO MUSEUM

larzanderson.org

Home to an excellent Anderson Motorcar Collection, as well as revolving exhibits featuring rare automobiles and automobilia.

➕ See map ▷ 100 ✉ 15 Newton Street, Brookline ☎ 617/522-6547 🕐 Tue–Sun 10–4 🚇 Reservoir (Green line D), bus 51 💰 Inexpensive

Fall color at the Arnold Arboretum

PLYMOUTH

The Pilgrims left Plymouth, England, for the New World on the *Mayflower*. After first stopping in Cape Cod, they made their way to Plymouth Harbor, which is commemorated on the waterfront by Plymouth Rock, the town having been named after the Devon port from where they set sail. Don't expect a boulder, however; most visitors are disappointed by the small size of the granite stone.

A more satisfying way to get in touch with the history of Massachusetts' first settlers is to visit them at Plimoth Plantation, a meticulously researched reproduction Pilgrim settlement 3 miles (5km) south. Here interpreters in period costume chat with visitors while getting on with their chores. The excellent curators work hard to make the village site accessible and display exhibits including how the Pilgrims' diet related to the seasons. At another exhibit, the Wampanoag Homesite, the Native Americans on whose ancestors' land the Pilgrims settled tell of their experiences. Also affiliated with the museum is the *Mayflower II*, a seaworthy replica of the ship that the Pilgrims sailed from England to the New World. Costumed interpreters provide below-decks tours and insight into the perilous crossing.

Plymouth is a popular destination and offers motels, restaurants and other attractions catering to visitors—some of them authentic, others tacky. One worth a stop is the Pilgrim Hall Museum, which is full of impressive artifacts once owned by the Pilgrims, including furniture, clothing and armor. A reproduction of the 1636 Plimoth Grist Mill operates twice a week, using water power to mill organic corn, which is for sale. One of the best times to visit Plymouth is during Thanksgiving, when the town pulls out all the stops with a parade and other events—and modern-day Native Americans stage an annual protest they call the "National Day of Mourning." Plymouth celebrates its 400th anniversary in 2020, marking the historic Mayflower Voyage and the founding of Plymouth Colony.

THE BASICS

seeplymouth.com
Distance: 50 miles (80km)
Journey Time: 1 hour
☎ Plimoth Plantation: 508/746-1622
🕐 Plimoth Plantation and *Mayflower II:* late Mar–Nov
🚆 From South Station
👆 Plimoth Plantation, *Mayflower II:* expensive. Pilgrim Hall Museum: moderate
ℹ Destination Plymouth
✉ 134 Court Street
☎ 508/747-7533

HIGHLIGHTS

● Plimoth Plantation
● The Wampanoag Homesite
● The *Mayflower II*
● Plymouth Rock
● Pilgrim Hall Museum

FARTHER AFIELD EXCURSIONS

LEXINGTON AND CONCORD

These lovely towns are immortalized by events that sparked the first shots of the Revolution. It was to Lexington, where Patriot leaders were staying, that Paul Revere made his famous ride to warn of British plans to seize a cache of arms in Concord. It was on Concord's North Bridge, on April 19, 1775, that the "shot heard round the world" was fired. Concord has a literary past, too, as the home of influential early 19th-century writers and thinkers Henry David Thoreau, Ralph Waldo Emerson, Nathaniel Hawthorne and Louisa May Alcott. Visit their houses, and their graves in Sleepy Hollow Cemetery. The Minute Man Visitor Center (open April through November) is an excellent place to start a visit.

SALEM

To many, Salem means witches, so it's not surprising to find a range of interpretations of the hysteria that hit the town in the 1690s.

The most popular attraction is the Salem Witch Museum, which treads a fine line between cheap thrills and historical accuracy in telling the macabre tale of the trials that claimed 19 lives. Other sites worth visiting are the Witch House, which belonged to the presiding judge, and the affecting memorial to the victims on Salem Common.

Less well known but far more striking once you're there is that the town also has a rich maritime history and some of the best Federal architecture in America. In the 18th and early 19th centuries Salem's prosperous shipbuilders, merchants and sea captains built graceful houses and filled them with beautiful things. Many of these objects are in the Peabody Essex Museum. Another not-to-miss site is The House of the Seven Gables, widely known as the setting of Nathaniel Hawthorne's 1851 novel.

The places to rest your head around Boston range from family-run bed-and-breakfasts to elaborate, world-class hotels. The majority are a convenient walking distance from the major sights.

Where to Stay

Introduction

Boston has no shortage of places to stay, so you're sure to find something to suit your personal preferences for style and amenities.

Bed-and-Breakfasts and Inns
Bed-and-breakfasts are often run out of a private home. They normally include a modest bedroom, plus a home-cooked breakfast, at a reasonable price. Boston and Cambridge have a number of such establishments in the city. A bit more luxurious and larger than a bed-and-breakfast, the best inns around Boston are often housed in historic buildings or town houses. They also often include breakfast, though sometimes charge a separate fee. Most will offer complimentary WiFi, and if you're lucky, parking.

Boutique and Luxury Hotels
Over the last several years, a stable of chic, modern small hotels has cropped up. The majority offer stylish, contemporary design, interesting restaurants on the property and concierge services. They are mostly in and around downtown Boston. Scattered throughout Boston's most popular neighborhoods (from Back Bay and Downtown to Harvard Square), the area's luxury hotels cater to the traveler's every need and whim. Some offer quirky amenities (such as the authors' library in the lobby at Harvard Square's Charles Hotel) alongside services such as in-room massages and personal shoppers.

HISTORIC HOTELS

A handful of the city's most history-laden sites are also places you can stay the night. **The Omni Parker House** (▷ 111) is America's longest continuously operating luxury hotel. Opened in 1855, it was the meeting site of a literary group that included Ralph Waldo Emerson and Nathaniel Hawthorne. Later, its dining room gained a place in Boston history as the site of President (then Senator) John F. Kennedy's proposal to Jacqueline Bouvier. The **Fairmont Copley Plaza** (▷ 112) has witnessed many of Boston's grandest celebrations.

Budget Hotels

PRICES
Expect to pay between $75 and $150 per night for a budget hotel.

BUCKMINSTER HOTEL

bostonhotelbuckminster.com

A mainstay in Kenmore Square for more than 100 years, Buckminster is located steps from Fenway Park and offers a great value.

➕ 6E ✉ 645 Beacon Street ☎ 617/375-2524 🚇 Kenmore Square Station

CHANDLER INN

chandlerinn.com

A great option in the pricey South End, Chandler offers a great bargain, with modern, comfortable rooms, free WiFi, iPod docks, marble bathrooms and walk-in showers.

➕ H7 ✉ 26 Chandler Street ☎ 617/482-3450 or 800/842-3450 🚇 Back Bay Station

COLLEGE CLUB

thecollegeclubofboston.com

A gem of a B&B, the College Club is a comfortable, inexpensive place to stay and the rooms, traditional in style, are all charming. Three rooms have shared bathrooms. Breakfast is included and WiFi is free.

➕ G6 ✉ 44 Commonwealth Avenue 🚇 617/536 9510 🚇 Arlington

COMFORT INN

comfortinn.com

Situated close to the University of Massachusetts, Boston and the JFK Library, this bargain hotel offers a free airport shuttle, complimentary breakfast and WiFi, as well as an outdoor pool.

➕ Off map at K9 ✉ 900 Morrissey Boulevard, Dorchester ☎ 617/287-9200 🚇 JFK/U Mass, then half-hourly hotel shuttle bus 7am–10pm

THE INN AT LONGWOOD MEDICAL

innatlongwood.com

Located less than a mile from Fenway Park and the Museum of Fine Arts, the Inn is a convenient base to explore Boston.

➕ D9 ✉ 342 Longwood Avenue ☎ 617/731-4700 or 800/468-2378 🚇 Green line D to Longwood

NEWBURY GUEST HOUSE

newburyguesthouse.com

This inn offers Victorian-style rooms—32 in all—in three connected redbrick row houses. It is an excellent value and quite popular, so it's wise to book well in advance.

➕ G6 ✉ 261 Newbury Street, Back Bay ☎ 617/670-6000 or 800/437-7668 🚇 Copley, Hynes Convention Center

PORTER SQUARE HOTEL

theportersquarehotel.com

Located in lively part of Cambridge, this mid-sized boutique property offers great deals and an easy walk to bustling Harvard Square, as well as to the convenient subway.

➕ Off map at 1B ✉ 1924 Massachusetts Ave., Cambridge, Massachusetts ☎ 617/499-3399 🚇 Porter Square Subway

---

BED-AND-BREAKFAST
Double occupancy in bed-and-breakfast accommodation ranges from $90 to $180. Try the **Bed-and-Breakfast Agency of Boston**, a helpful, friendly agency that will find you accommodation in historic houses and restored waterfront lofts. Nightly, weekly, monthly and winter rates (✉ 47 Commercial Wharf ☎ 617/ 720-3540, 800/248-9262 or 0800 895 128 from the UK; boston-bnbagency.com).

Mid-Range Hotels

AMES BOSTON HOTEL

ameshotel.com

The Ames Building is a smart, luxury boutique hotel. The minimalist but luxurious interior contrasts with the 19th-century exterior. Guest can make use of the smart fitness center.

🚇 K5 ✉ 1 Court Street ☎ 617/979-8100 🚇 Government Center

BEACON HILL HOTEL AND BISTRO

beaconhillhotel.com

Twelve tasteful rooms in two linked townhouses in the heart of Beacon Hill makes this a wonderful place to stay. The Bistro downstairs and the roof deck are nice perks.

🚇 H5 ✉ 25 Charles Street ☎ 617/723-7575 or 888/959-2442 🚇 Charles/MGH

COLONNADE

colonnadehotel.com

Behind the bland 1960s facade of this Back Bay hotel are large, comfortable rooms with free WiFi and complimentary bottled water. It also boasts the city's only rooftop pool.

🚇 F7 ✉ 120 Huntington Avenue, Back Bay ☎ 617/ 424-7000 or 800/962-3030 🚇 Prudential

CONSTITUTION INN

constitutioninn.org

Within sight of its namesake ship, this spartan, nautically themed inn offers both a great location and lots of perks, such as free WiFi and a local shuttle.

🚇 K2 ✉ 150 3rd Avenue, Charlestown ☎ 617/241-8400 🚇 North Station

ELIOT

eliothotel.com

Its Commonwealth Avenue address gives away the fact that this hotel is a beauty. The neo-French Empire-style boutique hotel, built in 1925, offers an elegant place to rest your head.

🚇 E6 ✉ 370 Commonwealth Avenue, Back Bay ☎ 617/ 267-1607 or 800/44 ELIOT 🚇 Hynes Convention Center

GRYPHON HOUSE

innboston.com

Tiny, but elegant, this inn, where each of the eight rooms are well-appointed, certainly has its own distinct identity. It is a lovely place to stay and is convenient for Back Bay.

🚇 E6 ✉ 9 Bay State Road ☎ 617/375-9003 🚇 Kenmore

HAMPTON INN & SUITES BOSTON CROSSTOWN CENTER

bostonhamptoninn.com

This is a modern-feeling and good value option at the edge of South End. It offers a free shuttle to many attractions.

🚇 F7 ✉ 811 Massachusetts Avenue ☎ 617/445-6400 🚇 Massachusetts Avenue (Orange line)

HARBORSIDE INN

harborsideinnboston.com

A downtown location and elegant furnishings make this hotel good value for the money. Rooms come with free HBO and a movie library, perfect for when sightseeing has tired you out.

🚇 K5 ✉ 185 State Street ☎ 617/723-7500 🚇 State

HOTEL MARLOWE

hotelmarlowe.com

An elegant hotel that although big has a boutique feel to it. Rooms are lushly

decorated and the service is excellent. Some rooms have fantastic views.

➕ H3 ✉ 24 Edwin Land Boulevard
☎ 617/868-8000 or 800/825-7140
Ⓣ Lechmere

HOTEL VERITAS

thehotelveritas.com

This independently owned hotel is ideal for exploring Cambridge. The rooms have a serene and luxurious feel.

➕ B2 ✉ 1 Remington Street, Cambridge
☎ 617/515 3390 Ⓣ Harvard

HYATT REGENCY BOSTON

regencyboston.hyatt.com

Family- and pet-friendly, this large hotel is close to Faneuil Hall and the Theater District. Muted tones and modern furnishings make for a comfortable stay.

➕ J6 ✉ One Avenue de Lafayette
☎ 617/912-1234 or 800/492-8804
Ⓣ Downtown Crossing

JEWEL OF NEWBURY

jewelboston.com

Take an exotic vacation-within-a-vacation with the eye-popping array of global antiques at this intimate Back Bay B&B.

➕ F7 ✉ 254 Newbury Street ☎ 617/536-5523 Ⓣ Hynes Convention Center

KENDALL HOTEL

kendallhotel.com

A former firehouse, close to MIT and just over the bridge to Boston has been converted into a boutique hotel, complete with Americana furnishings.

➕ F4 ✉ 350 Main Street, Cambridge
☎ 866/566-1300 Ⓣ Kendall

MARY PRENTISS INN

maryprentissinn.com

A large, antiques-filled bed-and-breakfast in an 1843 mansion with modern amenities. The rooms are beautifully presented and bursting with charm.

➕ E9 ✉ 6 Prentiss Street ☎ 617/661-2929
Ⓣ Porter

OMNI PARKER HOUSE

omnihotels.com

Historic and stately, this 19th-century hotel, near Boston Common, offers an elegant place to stay, with a rich wealth of Boston's past on display. Famous names associated with the hotel include almost every American president; Charles Dickens did the first reading of *A Christmas Carol* in America here; Ho Chi Minh worked as a baker in the kitchen; Malcolm X worked as a busboy; and President John F. Kennedy proposed to Jackie Bouvier in the restaurant. The Parker House roll and Boston cream pie were invented here.

➕ J5 ✉ 60 School Street, Downtown
☎ 617/227-8600 or 800/843-6664 Ⓣ Park Street

SHERATON BOSTON

starwood.com/sheraton

Enormous and convenient, with two towers connected by interior walkways to the Pru and Hynes. It caters to business travelers, but is also family-friendly.

➕ G7 ✉ Prudential Center, 39 Dalton Street ☎ 617/236-2000 or 888/627-7054
Ⓣ Prudential, Hynes Convention Center

THE VERB HOTEL

theverbhotel.com

Located in the Fenway area, this ultra-hip retro motel actually was a late 1950s motel. Upgraded with funky decor paying homage to the area's musical roots, it features pop memorabilia on the walls and lots of other fun elements.

➕ E6 ✉ 1271 Boylston Street ☎ 617/566-4500 Ⓣ Kenmore Square Station

Luxury Hotels

BOSTON HARBOR
bhh.com

A large, modern and elegant hotel on the waterfront. It's worth paying a little more for harbor views. There are also good views from the lovely restaurant.
➕ L5 ✉ 70 Rowes Wharf ☎ 617/439-7000 or 800/752-7077 🚇 Aquarium

BOSTON PARK PLAZA
bostonparkplaza.com

After a $100 million renovation, this iconic hotel, built in 1927, is a gorgeous spot to stay. Its location near the Public Garden and Theater District is ideal.
➕ H6 ✉ 64 Arlington Street ☎ 617/426-2000 or 800/225-2008 🚇 Arlington

COPLEY SQUARE
copleysquarehotel.com

This historic boutique hotel in the Back Bay offers a European feel, with elegant well-appointed rooms.
➕ G6 ✉ 47 Huntington Avenue, Back Bay ☎ 617/ 536-9000 or 800/225-7062 🚇 Copley

FAIRMONT COPLEY PLAZA
fairmont.com

A "grand dame" of Boston, with sumptuous decor and home to one of the best hotel bars, the OAK Long Room, in the city.
➕ G6 ✉ 138 St. James Avenue, Back Bay ☎ 617/267-5300 or 866/540-4417 🚇 Copley

FOUR SEASONS
fourseasons.com/boston

Top-notch elegance and service is the standard at this high-end property, which doesn't disappoint. Guests can also enjoy fine dining in The Bristol restaurant (▷ 61).
➕ H6 ✉ 200 Boylston Street, Back Bay ☎ 617/338-4400 or 800/332-3442 🚇 Arlington

LANGHAM HOTEL
langhamhotels.com

Once the Federal Reserve Bank, this historic hotel oozes luxury and refinement. It offers a unique, for Boston, afternoon tea served in the lobby's Reserve restaurant and Champagne Bar.
➕ K5 ✉ 250 Franklin Street ☎ 617/451-1900 🚇 State, Downtown Crossing

LENOX
lenoxhotel.com

Intimate and refined, this privately owned hotel in Back Bay offers a luxurious retreat from the hustle and bustle of the city. The service is excellent.
➕ G6 ✉ 710 Boylston Street ☎ 617/536-5300 or 800/225-7676 🚇 Copley

THE LIBERTY HOTEL
libertyhotel.com

Once a grim city jail, The Liberty was brilliantly transformed into a stunning contemporary hotel with river views. There's just enough tongue-in-cheek reference to its past with details such as keys, scales of justice and a restaurant called Clink. to be fun.
➕ H4 ✉ 215 Charles Street ☎ 617/224-4000 or 866/507-5245 🚇 Charles/MGH

NINE ZERO
ninezero.com

When the stars are in town, they stay at this chic boutique hotel on the Freedom Trail. Rooms have all the latest gadgets and amenities.
➕ J6 ✉ 90 Tremont Street ☎ 617/772-5800 🚇 Park Street

This section contains practical advice and information about getting to Boston and traveling around once you are there, as well as tips, useful phone numbers, money matters and public holidays.

Need to Know

Planning Ahead

When to Go

Summer and fall are peak visiting seasons. Hotels are busy at graduation time (May, June) and rates go up. In October you will get a glimpse of New England's fall foliage (better still farther north). The time between Thanksgiving and New Year is full of seasonal festivities.

TIME

Boston is on Eastern Standard Time, five hours behind GMT, three hours ahead of Los Angeles.

AVERAGE DAILY MAXIMUM TEMPERATURES

JAN	FEB	MAR	APR	MAY	JUN	JUL	AUG	SEP	OCT	NOV	DEC
37°F	37°F	46°F	56°F	66°F	76°F	82°F	80°F	75°F	63°F	52°F	37°F
3°C	3°C	8°C	13°C	19°C	24°C	28°C	27°C	24°C	17°C	11°C	3°C

Spring (April through May) is unpredictable, but can be wonderful, with cool nights and fresh days. This is when you can catch the magnolia blossoms in Back Bay.

Summer (June through August) is normally pleasantly warm, but occasional heatwaves can see temperatures soaring into the 90s.

Fall (September through November) is warm in September and crisp in October and November, when the foliage is at its most colorful.

Winter (December through March) is very cold. Even when the sky is blue winds can be biting. Snows regularly transforms the city; a slushy, gray mess inevitably follows.

WHAT'S ON

January *Martin Luther King weekend.*

February *Chinese New Year* (Jan/Feb).

March *Spring Flower Show. St. Patrick's Day Parade.*

April *Patriots' Day* (3rd Mon): Revere's Ride is recreated.

Boston Marathon (3rd Mon). *Kite Festival* (or May): held in Franklin Park.

May *May Fair* in Harvard Square.

Boston Pops Concerts.

June *Battle of Bunker Hill*: re-enactment (Sun before Bunker Hill Day, Jun 17).

Cambridge River Festival: Events on the river.

July *Boston Pops Concerts. Independence celebrations* (week of Jul 4): Boston Pops concert with fireworks, Boston Harborfest music festival and USS *Constitution* turnaround.

St Anthony's Feast (Jul/Aug weekends): North End.

August *Moon Festival*: Processions in Chinatown.

September *Boston Arts Festival*: Columbus Waterfront.

Boston Symphony Orchestra: Season Sep–May.

October *Columbus Day Parade.*

Head of the Charles Regatta (3rd week).

November *Christmas tree lighting ceremonie*s: Faneuil Hall Marketplace and Charles Square, Cambridge.

Boston Ballet—The Nutcracker (Nov–Dec): Boston Opera House.

December *Tree lighting ceremonies*: Prudential Center, Harvard Square.

Boston Tea Party (mid-Dec): Re-enactment.

Carol concert: Trinity Church. *First Night*: New Year's Eve.

Boston Online

boston.com
The *Boston Globe*'s website has the daily newspaper, with local news, listings and restaurant reviews.

boston.citysearch.com
A guide to local events, theater productions, movies, concerts, sports, stores and restaurants. The site tends to feature the big-name destinations and happenings, so you'll find everything from top-10 restaurant lists and heavy-hitter museum exhibits to addresses, phone numbers, schedules and maps.

bostonmagazine.com
As well as the monthly glossy magazine found around the city, you'll find loads of information on its website, from feature articles to restaurant reviews.

bostonusa.com
Run by the Greater Boston Convention and Visitors Bureau, this site includes details about attractions, events, hotels and the subway, as well as other useful visitor information.

cambridge-usa.org
This is the Cambridge Office for Tourism's site and it contains listings of hotels, restaurants, attractions and arts and entertainment venues, as well as an events calendar and general visitor information for the City of Cambridge.

digboston.com
This alt-weekly paper and website features local news, arts, music, food, movies and shopping. It's great for a more "local" angle.

mbta.com
The website of the MBTA (Massachusetts Bay Transportation Authority) is the place to look for timetables, maps and fare information for the T (subway), as well as commuter rail services and buses.

TRAVEL SITES

fodors.com
A complete travel-planning site. You can research prices and weather; book air tickets, cars and rooms; ask questions (and get answers) from fellow travelers; and find links to other sites.

massvacation.com
Visitor information from the Massachusetts Office of Travel and Tourism. The site includes an accommodation booking service.

orbitz.com
An air-fare search engine owned by five US airlines. It frequently offers low-fare specials.

discovernewengland.org
This is the official site for the states of New England, if you are planning a visit beyond Boston.

STAYING CONNECTED

Hopping on the internet is easy; many cafés in Back Bay (particularly on Newbury Street) offer free wireless services, as do many shops. The city also offers Wicked Free Wi-Fi, an outdoor wireless network, which is a still a work in progress. The service set identifier (SSID) is "WickedFreeWiFi." The Boston Public Library and the entire downtown Salem has WiFi.

Getting There

ENTRY REQUIREMENTS

International travelers going to the US under the Visa Waiver Program (VWP) are now subject to enhanced security requirements. Online completion and approval of ESTA (Electronic System for Travel Authorization), along with payment of the fee, is mandatory ahead of travel for all VWP travelers. For full details, go to https://esta.cbp.dhs.gov.

CAR RENTAL

Logan Airport has several rental companies

Alamo
alamo.com
☎ 877/222-9075

Avis
avis.com
☎ 800/633-3469

Budget
budget.com
☎ 800/218-7992

Dollar
dollar.com
☎ 800/800-4000

Enterprise
enterprise.com
☎ 800/325-8007

Hertz
hertz.com
☎ 800/654-3131

National
nationalcar.com
☎ 877/222-9058

Thrifty
thrifty.com
☎ 800/847-4389

AIRPORTS

Logan Airport is surrounded by the Boston Harbor on three sides, it has four terminals. Regional airports include T. F. Green Airport (Rhode Island), Manchester Airport (New Hampshire) and Worcester Airport (Massachusetts).

FROM LOGAN AIRPORT

For general airport information call 800/235-6426. "Massport Shuttle" buses run every 20 minutes (5.30am–1am; free) from every terminal to Airport subway (T) station; from here it's a few minutes' journey to central Boston ($2.75).

Taxis cost $25–$45 (including a tunnel toll, but not tip). Thanks to the new Massachusetts Turnpike extensions from Logan, travel time to and from the airport has been reduced dramatically. Allow roughly 15–25 minutes to or from Back Bay (▷ panel, opposite).

Harbor Express (tel 617/222-6999) is an exciting way to arrive. It's a 10-minute boat ride between Logan and Long Wharf in the Financial District, where you can pick up a taxi. Harbor Express also operates between Logan and Quincy and Hull, on the south shore (Mon–Fri 6.25am–10.35pm, only operates on weekends in the summer.; $9.25 to Long Wharf). An on-call City Water Taxi (tel 617/422-0392) runs all year from Logan to 15 different waterfront locations (Mon–Sat 6.30am–10pm, Sun 6.30am–8pm; $12). Shuttle buses connect all terminals with the water taxis.

OTHER AIRPORTS
Regional airports include T.F. Green Airport, Rhode Island (tel 401/737-8222); Manchester Airport, New Hampshire (tel 603/624-6539); and Worcester Airport, Massachusetts (tel 508/799-1350). It's then more than an hour's bus ride to Boston.

ARRIVING BY BUS
Greyhound (tel 800/231-2222) and Peter Pan Bus Lines (tel 800/343-9999) travel between New York and Boston's South Station, and (less frequently) to the rest of the USA and Canada.

ARRIVING BY CAR
Boston can be a difficult city to drive in for visitors, and parking is scarce. If you do drive, select a hotel with free parking, get a good map and plan your route.

The major east–west highway into Boston is the I-90 toll road, also known as the Massachusetts Turnpike. I-90 links up with I-93 just south of Downtown. I-93 is the major north–south highway, and it travels through tunnels under downtown Boston. I-95, the East Coast's major north–south interstate highway, circles the perimeter of the Boston metropolitan area.

ARRIVING BY TRAIN
Amtrak (tel 800/872-7245; amtrak.com) runs a frequent service between Boston's South Station and Providence, New York, Philadelphia and Washington, D.C. The high-speed Acela service between New York and Boston takes three and a half hours. South Station also serves Washington, D.C. and Chicago. Amtrak's Downeaster travels up the coast to Maine from North Station.

Trains running within New England tend to arrive and depart on time, but those traveling longer distances are frequently delayed—particularly in winter, when snow slows them down—usually anything from 10 minutes to an hour.

TIME TO LOGAN
From downtown Boston, driving to Logan averages 20 minutes. However, during heavy traffic hours (generally 7.30–9.30am and 4.30–6pm on weekdays), count on the ride taking 30 minutes, possibly even 40 in the dead of rush hour. Security lines on international flights can also be quite long, so plan accordingly.

EATING ON THE RUN
At Logan Airport, find:
Legal Sea Foods (you can also buy live lobsters to take home with you).
Wolfgang Puck, quick and healthy pizzas.
Todd English's Bonfire, new American cooking from one of New England's top chefs.
Boston Beer Works, micro-brews and American food.
Johnny Rockets, American burgers and shakes and a jukebox.
Fresh City, wrap sandwiches to go.
In South Station, find:
Tavern in the Square, drinks and bar food.
Au Bon Pain, sandwiches, soups and salads.
Regina Pizzeria, locally loved, small Italian chain.
Surf City Squeeze, for fresh-made fruit smoothies.

NEED TO KNOW GETTING THERE

Getting Around

BICYCLES

Boston has a bike-sharing program called Hubway, with 1,600 bikes for rent around the city (www.the-hubway.com). Boston has several bicycle paths that offer pleasant riding. One is the Southwest Corridor, which runs from behind the Massachusetts Avenue T stop as far as the Arnold Arboretum in Jamaica Plain. A longer ride is the Minuteman Bikeway, which runs from Alewife Station in Cambridge all the way out to Bedford—all passing by the historical sites in Lexington (▷ 106) on the way.

VISITORS WITH DISABILITIES

All Massport shuttle buses feature low floors for easier boarding, luggage racks, and are equipped with wheelchair lifts.
Public buildings, parking areas and most subway stations provide wheelchair access, and many hotels have specially designed rooms. Modern or newly renovated hotels and restaurants tend to be better equipped. For further information contact: New England INDEX ✉ 200 Trapelo Road, Waltham, MA 02452 ☎ 781/642-0248; disabilityinfo.org

VISITOR PASSES

● An MBTA (Massachusetts Bay Transportation Authority) Link Pass gives unlimited travel for one or seven days ($12, $21.25) on all subways, buses and ferries. It is available at vending machines in T stations and online in advance at mbta.com. It is NOT available at visitor information centers.

BOATS

● MBTA ferry/Boston Harbor cruises (tel 617/227-4321) link Long Wharf and Charlestown, Long Wharf and Provincetown.

BUSES

● Buses travel farther out into the suburbs than the T, but the T is much quicker and easier in the center.
● Passengers must have the exact change ($2) or Charlie Card. Express Bus has an additional charge.
● For travel farther afield, bus companies operate out of South Station and serve destinations throughout New England.

SUBWAY (T)

● Boston's system of subway and elevated trains is known as the T. The five lines—Red, Green, Orange, Silver and Blue—meet in central Boston. "Inbound" and "Outbound" refer to direction in relation to Park Street Station.
● The clean and efficient trains run from 5am (later on Sunday) to 1am.
● Rides are by Charlie Tickets (more expensive) or Charlie Cards, reloadable cards bought at vending machines in stations. Individual rides are $2.75 (ticket) or $2.25 (card). These machines are not especially easy for the first-time user, so it is a good idea to visit mbta.com in advance, for a clear explanation of the options and operation of machines.
● Free maps are available at the Park Street Station information booth. There is also a T map on the inside flap at the front of this book.

TAXIS

● Hail taxis on the street or find them at hotels and taxi stands.
● 24-hour taxi services include:
Bay State Taxi, call 617/566-5000
Metrocab Cab, call 617/782-5500
Boston Cab Association, call 617/536-5010

TRAINS

● MBTA commuter trains leave from North Station for destinations west and north, including Lowell, Concord, Salem, Manchester, Gloucester, Rockport and Ipswich. South Station serves Plymouth and Providence.

DRIVING AND CAR RENTAL
Car rental

● Rental drivers must be at least 21; many companies put the minimum age at 25 or charge extra for those between 21 and 25.
● For car rental companies, ▷ panel, 116.
● Consider using the subway to pick up your car from a rental agency on the outskirts of Boston to avoid having to drive in the city.

Driving

● Driving and parking in Boston is challenging.
● Park only in legal spots, or you will be towed. Park in the direction of the traffic.
● Speed limits on the major highways range from 55 to 65mph (89 to 105kph); elsewhere they range from 25 to 45mph (40 to 72kph).
● All passengers must wear a seat belt. Children under 12 years old must sit in the back and use an approved car seat or safety belt.
● You may turn right at a red traffic light if the road ahead is clear, unless signage prohibits it.
● Drink/driving laws are strict. Never drive after drinking; don't keep opened alcohol in the car.
● Look out for one-way streets, especially in downtown Boston where they are legion.
● Boston taxi drivers are aggressive—the best defense is to yield whenever necessary. And don't be afraid to use your horn.

PEDICABS

A fun and efficient alternative to taxis and subways are the "cycle rickshaws" run by Boston Pedicab (617/266-2005; bostonpedicab. com). The bicycle cabs are easy to find downtown and can take you to where you are going quickly.

TAXI FARES

At the time of publication, taxi rates are $2.60 for the first 1/7 mile (0.14km), and $0.40 for each additional 1/7 mile (0.14km); or $28 for each hour spent waiting. (Be sure to check rates at the airport.) Trips to and from the airport are subject to additional tolls of $2.75 and $5.25, respectively; there is no charge for luggage. For trips beyond 12 miles (19km) from downtown Boston, a flat-rate applies: cityofboston.gov

NEED TO KNOW GETTING AROUND

Essential Facts

TRAVEL INSURANCE

It is vital to have cover for medical expenses, as well as for theft, baggage loss, trip cancellation and accidents. Check your insurance coverage and buy a supplementary policy as needed.

MONEY

The currency is the dollar (=100 cents). Notes (bills) are in denominations of $1, $5, $10, $20, $50 and $100; coins are 25¢ (a quarter), 10¢ (a dime), 5¢ (a nickel) and 1¢ (a penny). You may find that small businesses will not break a $100, $50 or even $20 bill.

ALCOHOL

● It is illegal to drink alcohol in public places such as the T. Do not keep opened bottles of alcohol in the car.

● It is illegal to sell alcohol to anyone under the age of 21. Alcohol is on sale daily.

● Massachusetts prohibits Happy Hours, so don't look for any discounted drink specials at bars or restaurants.

MAGAZINES AND NEWSPAPERS

● Free tourist magazines are found in hotel lobbies, and include discount coupons.

● Listings can be found in the *Boston Globe* (Thursday), the *Boston Herald* (Friday) and *DigBoston*.

● *Boston Magazine* (monthly) reviews the Boston scene and gives awards to restaurants. Also online: bostonmagazine.com.

MAIL

● Letter boxes are gray/blue and have swing-top lids. Most hotels will mail letters for you.

MONEY MATTERS

● Nearly all banks have Automatic Teller Machines. Cards registered in other countries that are linked to the Cirrus or Plus networks are accepted. Before leaving, check which network your cards are linked to and ensure your PIN is valid in the US, where four-figure numbers are the norm.

● Credit cards are widely accepted.

● US dollar traveler's checks function like cash in larger hotels and stores.

● Money and traveler's checks can be exchanged at most banks (check fees as they can be high) and most travel centers.

● Some businesses may ask for photo identification before cashing traveler's checks.

LOST AND FOUND

● To report lost credit cards:
American Express ☎ 800/528-4800;
Diners Club/Carte Blanche ☎ 800/234-6377;

MasterCard ☎ 800/627-8372;
Visa ☎ 800/847-2911
● Lost traveler's checks:
American Express ☎ 800/221-7282

OPENING HOURS
● Banks: Mon–Fri 9–4, Thu 9–5 or later, Sat 9–12.
● Shops: Mon–Sat 10–6 or later. Sun mornings from 11am.
● Museums and sights: Unless otherwise stated, all sights mentioned in this book close on Thanksgiving and Christmas.
● Businesses: Mon–Fri 8 or 9–5.

PUBLIC HOLIDAYS
● Jan 1 (New Year's Day)
● 3rd Mon in Jan (Martin Luther King Day)
● 3rd Mon in Feb (President's Day)
● Last Mon in May (Memorial Day)
● July 4 (Independence Day)
● 1st Mon in Sep (Labor Day)
● 2nd Mon in Oct (Columbus Day)
● Nov 11 (Veterans Day)
● 4th Thu in Nov (Thanksgiving)
● Dec 25 (Christmas Day)
● Boston also celebrates: Mar 17 (Evacuation Day); 3rd Mon in Apr (Patriots' Day); Jun 17 (Bunker Hill Day).

SENSIBLE PRECAUTIONS
● Boston is basically a safe city, but it is wise to stick to well-lit and well-populated areas after dark. Avoid the lower half of Washington Street and Boston Common late at night.
● Discuss your itinerary with your hotel's reception staff so they can point out any potential problems. Be aware of the people around you, especially at night or in quiet areas.
● Keep your wallet or purse and mobile phone out of sight and don't carry valuables openly.
● Do not carry easily snatched bags and cameras, or put your wallet into your back pocket.
● Keep valuables in your hotel's safe and never carry more money than you need.

SMOKING
● Smoking is banned in restaurants. It is banned in many public places, including the T. Some hotels have no-smoking floors.
● Cambridge is by law smoke-free.

PARKING

If you plan on driving, note that the city is notorious for its lack of parking. That said, follow these tips, and you should do fine:

● Look for public parking garages. Though more costly, these are by far the most convenient, as they are plentiful (especially downtown). The garage under the Common is the most economical at $32 for 24 hours, $12 for additional hours.

● Allow extra time. Some destinations have garages and/or valet, some don't. If the latter, circle until you get lucky enough to find an empty spot on the street. Look for side streets but be careful not to park in "residents only" streets (which are the majority).

● Pay attention to parking signs—the meter officers are merciless.

● Lost traveler's checks are relatively quick and easy to replace. Keep the numbers of the checks separate from the checks themselves.

● Report any stolen item to the nearest police station, if only to be able to claim on your insurance. The police will fill out the forms your insurance company will need.

STUDENT TRAVELERS

● To get discounts on the T and admissions, get an International Student Identity Card (ISIC). If you are not a student but are under 26, get the International Youth Travel Card (IYTC).

● The Council on International Educational Exchange (CIEE) has a travel service offering domestic passes for bargain travel within the US. It is also the exclusive agent for several student-discount cards: 300 Fore Street, Portland, Maine, call 888/268-6245.

● Members of the Youth Hostel Association of England and Wales (Trevelyan House, Dimple Road, Matlock, Derbyshire DE4 3YH, call 01629 592600) can use Hi-Boston hostels.

● Information on student hostels within the US can be obtained from Hostelling International–USA (8401 Colesville Road, Suite 600, Silver Spring, MD 20910, call 240/650-2100; email: info@hihostels.com; hihostels.com).

TELEPHONES

● The area codes for Boston and Cambridge are 617 and 857. These must be included even when making local calls. Some communities outside the city have different area codes.

● To call the US from the UK dial 00 1, followed by the area code and the number.

● To call the UK from the US, dial 011 44, then drop the initial zero from the area code.

TICKETS

● The nine-day Boston CityPASS (adult $56; seniors and children ages 3–11 $44) gives free admission for one visit each at five key sights: the Museum of Science (▷ 28–29), the New England Aquarium (▷ 53), either the Boston

Harbor Cruise or Harvard Museum of Natural History (▷ 89), and Skywalk Observatory (▷ 73). Available from the above sights or at the visitor information center on Boston Common (▷ 50), in the Prudential Center (▷ 73) or online: citypass.com/city/boston.

TOURIST OFFICES

● Greater Boston Convention & Visitors Bureau Inc. 2 Copley Place, Suite 105, Boston, MA 02116 (tel 617/ 536-4100; bostonusa.com).
● Massachusetts Office of Travel & Tourism State Transportation Building, 10 Park Plaza, Suite 4510, Boston, MA 02116 (tel 617/973-8500; massvacation.com).
● Boston National Historical Park Visitor Center Located in Faneuil Hall (tel 617/242-5601).
● Boston Common Visitor Center, 139 Tremont Street (tel 617/426-3115).
● Cambridge Office for Tourism, 4 Brattle Street, Harvard Square, Cambridge (tel 617/441-2884; cambridgeusa.org).

EMERGENCY MEDICAL TREATMENT	
Ambulance, fire, police	☎ 911
Massachusetts General Hospital	☎ 617/726-2000
Inn House Doctor	☎ 617/859-1776 ◷ 24 hours. Makes hotel visits
Late-night pharmacies: CVS	✉ Porter Square (35 White Street, near Massachusetts Avenue), Cambridge ☎ 617/876-5519 ◷ 24 hours
	✉ 587 Boylston Street, Back Bay ☎ 617/437-8414 ◷ 24 hours
Dental emergency	☎ 617/636-6828
Eye and Ear Infirmary	☎ 617/523-7900
Physician Referral Service	☎ 617/726-5800 ◷ Mon–Fri 8.30–4.45

CONSULATES	
Canada	✉ 3 Copley Place ☎ 617/247-51000
Great Britain	✉ 1 Broadway, Cambridge ☎ 617/245-4500
Ireland	✉ 535 Boylston Street ☎ 617/267-9330
Italy	✉ 600 Atlantic Avenue ☎ 617/722-9201
Portugal	✉ 699 Boylston Street ☎ 617/536-8740
Spain	✉ 31 St. James Avenue ☎ 617/536-2506

Timeline

REVOLUTION

In the 1760s Britain imposed taxes on her New England colonists. Increasingly angry at interference in their lucrative seafaring trade, the colonists, led by Sons of Freedom Samuel Adams and John Hancock, protested at having to pay taxes when they had no representation in the government that was taxing them. Tension began to mount and on March 5, 1770 British soldiers killed five colonists in what became known as the Boston Massacre. On December 16, 1773, Patriots protested against the Tea Act by throwing tea into the sea (the Boston Tea Party). British retaliation made clashes inevitable.

From left: American Revolution re-enactment; statue of a Minute Man on the spot where events sparked the revolution; plaque on the grave of Samuel Adams; equestrian statue of Paul Revere; obelisk commemorating the Battle of Bunker Hill, June 17, 1775

Pre-1620 The Algonquins inhabit the Boston area.

1620 Pilgrims arrive on the *Mayflower* and establish the first English colony in Plymouth.

1629 Puritans found the Massachusetts Bay Colony in Charlestown.

1630 The colony moves to Beacon Hill on the Shawmut Peninsula.

1636 Harvard College is founded.

1680 Most of Boston is concentrated in what is to become the North End, around the flourishing seaport.

1775 The Revolution starts in Boston.

1776 The British leave Boston on March 17. On July 18, the Declaration of Independence is read from the State House balcony.

1790s Trade with China brings prosperity.

1795 Architect Charles Bulfinch starts the new State House. Five years later he helps to develop Beacon Hill.

1826 Mayor Josiah Quincy extends the waterfront and builds Quincy Market.

1840s Irish immigrants, fleeing the Potato Famine, pour into the North End.

NEED TO KNOW TIMELINE

1856 Work begins on filling in and developing the Back Bay as a new residential area.

1897 The Boston Marathon is launched. John J. McDermott of New York wins.

1918 The Red Sox win baseball's World Series—their first pennant victory. Their next victory was not to be until 2004.

1960s-70s An extensive urban renewal scheme includes John Hancock Tower.

1990 The US's biggest art theft occurs at the Isabella Stewart Gardner Museum.

2004 New England Patriots win the Super Bowl for the second time since 2002. The Boston Red Sox win the World Series championship for the first time in almost a century.

2006 The Big Dig, Boston's decade-long, large-scale construction project to ease Boston's huge traffic problem, finally ends.

2013 The motto "Boston Strong" goes round the world after the April 15 Boston Marathon bombings that killed three and injured more than 250. The city's beloved Boston Red Sox respond by winning the World Series for the eighth time.

2020 Grand celebrations mark the 400th anniversary of the founding of Plymouth Colony and the arrival of the *Mayflower*.

PAUL REVERE'S RIDE

In his lifetime Paul Revere (1735–1818) was known as a silversmith, but he was immortalized—with some poetic license—as a hero of the Revolution by the poet Henry Wadsworth Longfellow. Revere was a messenger for the Sons of Liberty and on the eve of the first battle of the Revolution rode to Lexington to warn local militia men about British preparations.

JFK

John Fitzgerald Kennedy was born in the Boston suburb of Brookline in 1917. His grandfather, "Honey-Fitz," was one of a long line of Irish mayors. Kennedy was elected president in 1960—good-looking and charismatic, he was a symbol of the nation's hope for a progressive future. He was assassinated on November 22, 1963.

NEED TO KNOW TIMELINE

Index

Boston 25 Best

WRITTEN BY Sue Gordon
ADDITIONAL WRITING Alexandra Hall and Michael Blanding
UPDATED BY Kim MacKinnon
SERIES EDITOR Clare Ashton
COVER DESIGN Chie Ushio, Yuko Inagaki
DESIGN WORK Tom Whitlock and Liz Baldin
IMAGE RETOUCHING AND REPRO Ian Little

Published in the United Kingdom by AA Publishing

ISBN 978-1-64097-091-5

NINH EDITION

All details in this book are based on information supplied to us at press time. Always confirm information when it matters, especially if you're making a detour to visit a specific place. Fodor's expressly disclaims any liability, loss, or risk, personal or otherwise, that is incurred as a consequence of the use of any of the contents of this book.

Color separation by AA Digital Department
Printed and bound by Leo Paper Products, China

10 9 8 7 6 5 4 3 2 1

A05593
Maps in this title produced from mapping © MAIRDUMONT / Falk Verlag 2017 and data from openstreetmap.org © OpenStreetMap contributors
Transport map © Communicarta Ltd, UK

The AA would like to thank the following photographers, companies and picture libraries for their assistance in the preparation of this book.

2 AA/M Lynch; 3 AA/M Lynch; 4t AA/M Lynch; 4c AA/M Lynch; 5t AA/M Lynch; 5c Kyle Klein (GBCVB); 6t AA/M Lynch; 6cl AA/C Sawyer; 6c AA/M Lynch; 6cr AA/M Lynch; 6bl AA/C Sawyer; 6bcl AA/C Sawyer; 6bcr AA/C Coe; 6br Photodisc; 7t AA/M Lynch; 7cl AA/J Nicholson; 7cr AA/C Sawyer; 7bl AA/M Lynch; 7bc AA/J Nicholson; 7br AA/M Lynch; 8 AA/M Lynch; 9 AA/M Lynch; 10t AA/M Lynch; 10ct AA/C Sawyer; 10c AA/C Sawyer; 10/11cb AA/D Clapp; 10/11b AA/C Coe; 11t AA/M Lynch; 11ct AA/M Lynch; 11c AA/C Sawyer; 12 AA/M Lynch; 13t AA/M Lynch; 13tct AA/C Sawyer; 13ct AA/J Nicholson; 13c AA/D Clapp; 13cb Brand X Pictures; 13b AA/M Lynch; 14t AA/M Lynch; 14ct AA/C Sawyer; 14c AA/C Sawyer; 14cb AA/C Sawyer; 14b AA/C Sawyer; 15t AA/M Lynch; 16t AA/M Lynch; 16ct AA/M Lynch; 16cb AA/C Sawyer; 16b AA/J Nicholson; 17t AA/M Lynch; 17ct AA/C Sawyer; 17c AA/M Lynch; 17b AA/C Sawyer; 18t AA/M Lynch; 18ct AA/C Sawyer; 18c AA/J Nicholson; 18cb AA/C Sawyer; 18b AA/P Kenward; 19t AA/J Nicholson; 19ct AA/C Sawyer; 19c AA/J Nicholson; 19cb AA/C Coe; 19b AA/C Sawyer; 20/21 AA/D Clapp; 24tl AA/C Sawyer; 24cl AA/C Sawyer; 24cr AA/C Sawyer; 24/25t AA/C Coe; 24/25c AA/C Coe; 25r AA/J Nicholson; 26tl AA/C Sawyer; 26tr AA/J Nicholson; 26c GBCVB; 27 Kyle Klein (GBCVB) 28l AA/C Sawyer; 28/29t AA/C Sawyer; 28/9b AA/C Sawyer; 29tr Courtesy of Boston Museum of Science; 29bl AA/D Clapp; 29br AA/D Clapp, 30 AA/C Sawyer; 30/31 AA/C Sawyer; 31 AA/M Lynch; 32/3 McPhoto/ADR – Bildagentur-online/ Alamy Stock Photo; 33 AA/J Nicholson 34l AA/J Nicholson; 34c AA/C Sawyer; 34r AA/C Coe; 35l AA/J Nicholson; 35r AA/C Coe; 36 AA/C Coe; 36/37t AA/C Sawyer; 36/37b AA/J Nicholson; 37l AA/C Coe; 37r AA/J Nicholson; 38t AA/C Sawyer; 38bl Courtesy of Greater Boston Convention & Visitors Bureau; 38br AA/C Sawyer; 39t AA/C Sawyer; 39br Courtesy of Museum of African American History; 40 AA/J Nicholson; 41 AA/D Clapp; 42 AA/C Sawyer; 43 Digital Vision; 44 Photodisc ; 45 AA/C Sawyer; 46 AA/C Sawyer; 47 AA/D Clapp; 50 AA/M Lynch; 51 AA/C Sawyer; 52l Courtesy of Institute of Contemporary Art/Boston; 52r Courtesy of Institute of Contemporary Art/Boston; 53l AA/C Sawyer; 53r AA/C Sawyer; 54t AA/C Sawyer; 54b AA/C Sawyer; 55t AA/C Sawyer; 55b AA/C Sawyer; 56t AA/C Sawyer; 56bl Courtesy of Old South Meeting House; 56br AA/C Sawyer; 57 AA/J Nicholson; 58 AA/S McBride; 59 Digital Vision; 60 Brand X pictures; 61 AA/P Bennett; 62 Bananastock; 63 AA/C Coe; 66l AA/C Sawyer; 66r AA/C Sawyer; 67l AA/C Sawyer; 67r AA/C Coe; 68l GBCVB; 68r Marcio Silva/Alamy Stock Photo Stock Photo; 69l Courtesy of Isabella Stewart Gardner Museum; 69r Courtesy of Isabella Stewart Gardner Museum; 70 Courtesy of Museum of Fine Arts; 70/71 AA/C Sawyer; 72l AA/C Sawyer; 72r AA/C Sawyer; 73l AA/J Nicholson; 73c AA/C Sawyer; 73r AA/D Clapp; 74 AA/J Nicholson; 74/75 AA/J Nicholson; 76 AA/M Lynch; 76/77 AA/C Sawyer; 77 AA/C Sawyer; 78t AA/C Sawyer; 78b The Mary Baker Eddy Library; 79 AA/J Nicholson; 80 AA/C Sawyer; 81 AA/C Sawyer; 82 Photodisc; 83 Digital Vision; 84 Brand X Pictures; 85 AA/C Coe; 88 Eric Fowke/Alamy Stock Photo; 90l AA/M Lynch; 90/1l AA/M Lynch; 90/1b AA/M Lynch; 91t AA/C Coe; 91bl AA/C Sawyer; 91br AA/M Lynch; 91l AA/C Sawyer; 91r AA/C Sawyer; 92t AA/C Sawyer; 92bl AA/M Lynch; 92br AA/J Nicholson; 93 AA/J Nicholson; 94 AA/J Tims; 95 AA/C Sawyer; 96 Brand X Pictures; 97t Photodisc; 97c AA/D Clapp; 98 AA/T Souter; 99 AA/M Lynch; 102 Photolibrary; 103l Courtesy of Kennedy Presidential Library Museum; 103r Courtesy of Kennedy Presidential Library Museum; 104t AA/C Sawyer; 104b AA/C Sawyer; 105 AA/P Bennett; 106t AA/P Bennett; 106bl AA/J Lynch; 106bcl AA/C Coe; 106bc AA/C Coe; 106bcr AA/C Sawyer; 106br AA/J Lynch; 107 AA/C Sawyer; 108t AA/C Sawyer; 108ct AA/M Lynch; 108c AA/C Sawyer; 108cb AA/S McBride; 108b AA/C Sawyer; 109 AA/C Sawyer; 110 AA/C Sawyer; 111 AA/C Sawyer; 112 AA/C Sawyer; 113 AA/C Sawyer; 114 AA/C Coe; 115 AA/C Coe; 116 AA/C Coe; 117 AA/C Coe; 118 AA/C Coe; 119t AA/C Coe; 120 AA/C Coe; 121t AA/C Coe; 122 AA/C Coe; 123 AA/C Coe; 124t AA/C Coe; 124bl AA/J Lynch; 124br AA/C Sawyer; 125t AA/C Coe; 125bl AA/C Coe; 125bc AA/C Sawyer; 125br AA/C Sawyer

Every effort has been made to trace the copyright holders, and we apologise in advance for any accidental errors. We would be happy to apply the corrections in the following edition of this publication.

Titles in the Series